ONE WEEK L

D0542353

The *New Leaders*

Achieving Corporate Transformation through Dynamic Leadership

PAUL TAFFINDER

KOGAN
PAGE

YOURS TO HAVE AND TO HOLD
BUT NOT TO COPY

First published in 1995
Reprinted 1995
Paperback edition published 1997
Reprinted 1997

Kogan Page Limited
120 Pentonville Road
London N1 9JN

© Paul Taffinder, 1995

British Library Cataloguing in Publication Data

A CIP record for this book is available from the British Library.

ISBN 0 7494 1381 6

ISBN 0 7494 2229 7 pbk

Typeset by Kogan Page
Printed and bound in Great Britain by
Biddles Ltd, Guildford and King's Lynn

CONTENTS

TABLES

FIGURES

PREFACE

Leadership is one of those subjects about which almost everyone has an opinion. This is hardly a new phenomenon: I don't doubt that when our earliest ancestors were still dragging their knuckles in the dust, the leadership of this tribe or that hunting expedition occasioned not a few grunts around the campfire of an evening. Only partially further on in our understanding of human psychology, we are still grunting about leadership today.

Our concerns, as we approach the millenium, are multifarious and complex. The world seems a much smaller place, linked by all manner of networks – physical, economic, political and electronic. We delight in the advantages these bring, both at home and at work. But the affairs of our post-modern, digital, re-engineered and economically-advantaged world are still complicated by the same basic human issues that have so absorbed our forebears through every generation since the first campfire was lit. We fight wars over territory, poverty and resources. Nations still struggle for self-determination. We seek to impose trading arrangements most favourable to the countries we inhabit and vigorously protect our national interests. We strive to avoid the worst and gain the best – for ourselves, our industries and our businesses. We have done this down through the centuries, no matter what the circumstances, by investing faith, hope, authority and expectation in a few individuals whom we dignify with the title *leader*.

My own interest in leadership began when I started my doctoral research in psychology where I was attempting to understand the exercise of organizational control. No great academic stride is needed to see that the actions of leaders are, at the very least, the trigger for innumerable organizational events and consequences which may or may not count in the success or otherwise of an enterprise. My interests, however, took me, not further into academia, but into the business world where management and leadership seem a million miles away from the neat theories that abound in textbooks. Management as practised is (and I can think of no better way of putting it) messy. Leadership more so. We can describe and analyse it, but at best we only approximate its character and its impact. We face similar difficulties in trying to understand the effects produced by management and those produced by leadership. Exposed to not a few managers and leaders over my consulting career, increasingly I have come to think of leadership as qualitatively different from management behaviour. I have also reached a point of frustration at the inability of many organizations worldwide to develop leaders, rather than 'simply' high performance managers. Yet at the same time, genuinely effective leaders seem to pop up in firms, gigantic and globe-straddling or small, local and virtually unheard-of, almost in spite of their managerial careers.

These thoughts more and more have tended to occupy my musings and inform the work I do with organizations. A book seemed inevitable. At the very least, for me it answers some of the questions noted above, acknowledges the realities of what it means to be and become a leader and celebrates the achievements of those leaders with whom I have been fortunate enough to work. At best, it will encourage you to think about leadership in a different way, to recognize the difficulties of getting there, and perhaps encourage you to take the first step in a different, more challenging, more rewarding direction.

Paul Taffinder
London
April, 1995

ACKNOWLEDGEMENTS

My thanks are due to a number of people, not least the business leaders who gave of their time to participate in the research interviews for the book and made the findings meaningful by their considerable candour. I am indebted to them.

I also would like to express my thanks to a number of other people across the globe, many of them at Coopers & Lybrand, who supported, pulled strings, gave advice and otherwise assisted me during the research, shaping and completion of the book. In no particular order they are:

David Taylor, Angus Hislop, Roger Cooke, Lawrie Philpott, Bob Anthony, Don McCue, Derkjan van der Leest, Kelvin Hard, Jack de Kreij, Phineas Mogotsi, Bob Lindgren, Mike Stanton, Anne Burford, Louise Marshman, Elaine Colleran, Tracy Griffin, Anne Lee, Mike Lewis, Joyce Booler, Richard Pomerantz, Brian Carty, Laurie Goulding, Davin Chown and Conrad Viedge.

To

Mandy, for love and unstinting support,
and AJ, for barging in to type gibberish on the lap-top.

THE BUSINESS LEADERS

The individuals who participated in the research interviews for this book come from diverse backgrounds, industries and countries. They head enterprises and, in some cases, business units of varying size. In general their markets are different. Some of their organizations straddle the globe, operating in fifty or more countries. Several operate in only one. A number are responsible for hundreds of thousands of employees, others a few hundred. The differences between them greatly outweigh any similarities, but what they share is both significant and profound.

What they share, of course, is the requirement of leadership.

Hans Boom
Betuweroute: Project Manager of the Netherlands freight rail link between Rotterdam and Germany. Infrastructure costs of $4.4 billion.

Dave Bowyer
Megapak: Managing Director. $50 million turnover. 550 employees. Business: plastics converting (injection and blow-moulding). Part of the Sentrachem Group of South Africa.

John Clark
BET: Chief Executive. $3.16 billion turnover. 105,100 employees. Business: business services, distribution, plant, and textile services. Operates in Britain, continental Europe and North America.

Bill Cockburn
The Post Office (Britain): Chief Executive. $8.9 billion turnover. 200,000 employees. Operations: Royal Mail, Parcelforce and Post Office Counters.

Note: All business statistics are those available for the latest financial year, either 1993 or 1994.

Simon Dyer
The Automobile Association (Britain): Director General (also World President of the Alliance Internationale de Tourism). $916 million consolidated income. 14,600 employees. Operates in Britain and continental Europe.

Peter Ellwood
TSB Group plc: Chief Executive. $3.2 billion income. 27,500 employees. Business: retail banking and insurance, merchant banking and other financial services. Operates primarily in Britain.

John B McCoy
Banc One Corporation: Chairman and Chief Executive Officer. $6.4 billion turnover. 48,800 employees. Business: banking and other financial services (a multibank holding company owning more than 80 banks). Operates in 12 states in the US.

Junior Potloane
Nedcor (South Africa): General Manager (Personal Banking). $800 million income (Group). 15,200 employees. Group business: banking and other financial services. Operates primarily in South Africa.

Ian Preston
Scottish Power: Chief Executive. $2.5 billion turnover. 8300 staff. Business: electricity supply, electrical goods retailing, information systems and engineering services. Operates in Britain.

Koos Radebe
South African Broadcasting Corporation: General Manager (Commercial Radio). $350 million operating revenue (Group). 5200 employees. Business: public broadcasting. Operates in South Africa.

Nelson Robertson
General Accident: Group Chief Executive. $8 billion premium income. 23,000 employees. Business: all types and classes of general and long-term insurance and assurance. Operates in 40 countries, primarily Britain, the US, Canada, Australia, New Zealand, Asia and Europe.

Alexander J Trotman
Ford Motor Company: Chairman, President and Chief Executive Officer. $128 billion turnover. 336,000 employees. Business: manufacture, assembly and sale of cars and trucks; also financing, insurance, savings and loan operations and vehicle and equipment leasing. Operates worldwide but especially in the US, Canada, Britain, Germany, and Southern Europe.

Robert van Gelder
Royal Boskalis Westminster: Chairman. $570 million turnover. 2700 employees. Business: dredging, environmental services, engineering. Operates in Europe, Africa, Middle East, Asia, Pacific, Far East, Australasia, and Central and South America.

Alex Watson
Chep in Europe: President and Chief Executive Officer. 2000 employees. Business: pallet and container pooling. Over 30 million pallets in circulation. Operates in Britain, Eire, Belgium, Holland, France, Germany, Spain, and Portugal.

Derek Wanless
NatWest Group: Group Chief Executive. $11.2 billion income. 91,400 employees. Business: retail, corporate, investment banking and other financial services. Operates in Britain, the US, Western Europe, Asia and Australia.

WHERE HAVE ALL THE LEADERS GONE?

Standing above the Babble

At the conclusion of his monumental work *War and Peace*, Leo Tolstoy devoted 12 chapters to an analysis of power and leadership. Tolstoy was concerned about the perennial questions of how and why an individual got entire nations to do as he or she wished. He was seeking as much as anything, we must suppose, an explanation for the extraordinary, world-changing events to which his epic novel is directed – Napoleon Bonaparte's conquest of Europe and his invasion of Russia, the years in which millions of people's lives were profoundly affected by war and by peace.

So what's changed?

Not a lot by all accounts. The much talked-about peace dividend emerging from the Cold War's evaporation seems to have the blurred edges of a mirage. We see it in the distance because the politicians of the world tell us it's there, but nearer at hand are the realities of a blood-spattered Bosnia and Rwanda, the disaster in Somalia, the continued festering in Sadam Hussein's Iraq and in Palestine, and the confused Tomahawk foreign policy of the world's prominent nations.

In Tolstoy's time, in the early 1800s, people looked to the great leaders of the day for direction – Napoleon, Tsar Alexander, the Duke of Wellington, General Kutuzov. We, of course, do the same in the 1990s. But something *has* changed.

In 1993 *Time* magazine ran with the cover, 'What's happened to Leadership?' An absence of vision, protested *Time's* James Walsh, characterized the world's richest and most powerful democracies. That article proved telling indeed. Across the globe

The New Leaders

1994 was a year of leadership crises. In Japan, Kiichi Miyazawa was sent packing by an electorate revolting against 38 years of Liberal Democratic rule, and his victorious opponent Morihiro Hozokawa was obliged to resign only months later, followed, incredibly, by Tsutomu Hata, premier for only 57 days. Bill Clinton's fortunes have fared somewhat better: he is still in office, although he has taken the Democratic party, in former Defense Secretary Dick Cheney's words, 'to its lowest level in 50 years'. Having given up control of both chambers of the US Congress, he is still dogged by the embarrassment of *waffle, women and Whitewater* soundbites and, more crucially, by continuing foreign policy failures.

In France the 1995 elections brought to an end François Mitterrand's 14 years of Socialist rule, and across the English Channel opinion polls, European and local elections alike have savaged John Major, with members of his own party calling on him to step aside for a new leader. Helmut Kohl has had the lowest popularity rating among the top German politicians, narrowly escaping electoral defeat in 1994. In Italy the face of politics has changed out of all recognition as the old guard of career politicians have been ousted by the right wing (some would say fascist) coalition headed, amazingly, by a media tycoon, Silvio Berlusconi, himself the subject of corruption investigations and whose coalition collapsed in late 1994.

It is as if the great mass of people in the leading democracies were yearning for some unifying vision of the future, the kind of unifying vision once provided in response to the Soviet Union's dark threat. That human beings need a vision, a purpose, hardly needs stating, but it is as well to remind ourselves that this cliché of leadership is and doubtless always will be fundamental to the mobilization of a collective will. However, *how* the vision is provided is as important as the message. In *Shadows of Forgotten Ancestors* Carl Sagan and Ann Druyan, examining what it means to be human, put the case cogently:

> We crave a purpose to give meaning to our existence. We do not want to hear that the world was not made for us. We are unimpressed with moral codes contrived by mere mortals; we want one handed down from on high.
>
> *Sagan and Druyan, 1992, p6*

There is an important lesson here for the leaders of the world's prominent democracies. Gone are the decades of the 1950s and 1960s when the developed world experienced unusual stability, predictions could be made and policies would – obligingly – work. Try as they might to influence their economies or to engineer change in society, political leaders must know that their capacity to do so is very limited. But they do have the power to set the context for ordinary people's lives, to say what is important and what isn't, to paint a picture of an individual's place in history and in the direction of the country. 'A leader,' wrote Andrew Marr in one of London's leading broadsheets, 'must strive to convey to the people a sense of what is happening, some proportion, an overview … . A prime minister should be standing above the babble not … adding to the noise.' (*The Independent*, 15 April 1994)

The Death of Leadership?

Has leadership failed? Or worse, is it simply absent? Two years ago, Bill Clinton was widely seen as a youthful tribune of change and master of statecraft. Today, to all appearances, he is a President who struggles daily to convince others he is worthy of the office. Yet Americans are, on the whole, quite well off and secure – surpassingly so, by the standards of most of the world. West Europeans and Japanese are too. Europeans who used to live behind the Iron Curtain struggle with dodgier economic circumstances today, but they also have much freer societies and more accountable governments. Latin America is ticking along after generations of strong-arm caudillos or misguided leftists.

On a truly demoralized, economically blighted continent, South Africa's President Nelson Mandela is the one figure most people around the world could accept as a genuinely heroic, visionary leader. The idea of South Africa as a lamp unto nations would have seemed preposterous a few years ago, but its example may illuminate what depresses spirits elsewhere.

That is, the tragedy of many leaders today is perhaps the lack of tragedy. Says Anne Lauvergeon, Mitterrand's deputy chief of staff at the Elysee Palace: 'I think they all lack the grandeur of an epic period. Compared to Napoleon's time, what is the era we live in today? One of budgets and deficits and unemployment.' The sort of vision that uplifts public sights, one that forges a sense of shared goals and common sacrifices, thrives best in a climate of stark moral choices. Mandela still personifies the ideals of overcoming the clear brutality of racism.

Under communism, Vaclav Havel in Czechoslovakia and Lech Walesa in Poland were moral apostles; in office, after the dragon of tyranny vanished, they became merely fallible men.

In richer countries today, the largest dragons on the scene are invisible: an absence of new horizons, common causes and sheer competence to grab even the tail of this beast. Beyond that, leadership has to grapple with concerns of ocean-crossing reach and technological complexity that elude the sovereign powers of any one nation. Trade, investment, artistic and pop-culture movements, the flow of labor and natural resources – all seem to sway more and more with transnational tides. By objective, historical measures, a considerable number of countries have cause today to feel contented; instead, many of them feel a mounting sense of uncertainty, lack of control and vacuum of political vision.

James Walsh, 'The *Time* Global 100'
Time (4 December 1994, p24)
© 1994 *Time Magazine*. Reprinted with permission.

Leapfrogging and CyberSociety

We have begun this book on business leadership by glancing at some of the world's political leaders not to learn lessons necessarily from them but to understand first and foremost that the world in which they jockey for power and position has changed. What we see as leadership crises are the struggles of politicians to adapt to rapid and enormous social and economic shifts. Business leaders inhabit the same world. In the 1990s they too are on a world stage.

This fact could not be more stark than when we look at Peters and Waterman's *In Search of Excellence* (1982), the definitive work of the 1980s, the bible of management thinkers and MBA students and the guiding light to thousands of executives worldwide, who used its principles in the hope of emulating the success of the 'excellent companies'. IBM was one of those companies and one that had enjoyed the plaudits and envy of business people for 40 years. 'What our rational economist friends tell us ought not to be possible,' declared Peters and Waterman, 'the excellent companies do routinely' (1982, p xxii). Unfortunately what the old 'Big Blue', like many of the excellent companies, has done routinely in the early 1990s is to lose billions of dollars. From $6 billion profit in 1990, IBM crumbled to a $5 billion loss in 1992, putting the brakes on its abrupt slide from global pre-eminence only by dint of the harshest organizational cutting and slicing.

What is most interesting about Peters and Waterman's original work is the confirmation that at the heart of the excellent companies was the ubiquitous driving force of a strong leader. But perhaps this too was their fundamental weakness. Very powerful leaders, with unflinching values embedded into everything an organization does, will find it immensely difficult, not to see the necessity for change, but to discover how to change. IBM's John Akers, abdicating power in March 1993, is one of these.

Across the Atlantic in Europe, Daimler-Benz epitomizes this in the 1990s. Aggressive expansion under outgoing chief executive Edzard Reuter has brought the company from a car-based German business of a decade ago to a global integrated technology group whose turnover has doubled in that time to $60 billion. The group has fingers in several pies, including aerospace, trains and power equipment. But Reuter's leadership also brought Daimler's first post-war loss in 1993 of $1.1 billion through restructuring costs and lack of synergy between subsidiaries. In his place comes Jurgen Schrempp, picked for his broad international experience and his success in hammering through a brutal transformation of Deutsche Aerospace, Daimler's aerospace subsidiary.

Indeed the international dimension and the need for active business transformation are the two elements that characterize the difficulties faced by Schrempp and leaders like him. For Daimler-Benz competition in almost all their markets has become intense, with the new Mercedes C-class cars, for example, having to be sold at average prices 10 per cent lower than Mercedes hoped to achieve. Moreover, the assumption no longer holds that organizations can 'go through' fundamental change via some kind of business re-engineering and expect to arrive, having leapfrogged their competitors, at a new equilibrium. The painful adjustments of re-engineering and cost-cutting (such as Mercedes' planned shedding of 42,500 jobs between 1992 and 1995) are no guarantee of success in a company's international or even local markets.

Mazda, the Japanese car-maker, loss-making in 1993 and 1994 for the first time in 19 years, is just beginning to come to terms with this. The usual things have been happening there: a 10 per cent reduction in heads from the 30,000 complement, determined efforts to seek cost-savings from the redesign of components (via a near doubling of its design engineering department), and intense negotiation with suppliers to get price cuts of 10 per cent. All well and good, but at the same time Henry Wallace and two other senior Ford executives, appointed to Mazda in the last year as part of the 25-year-old partnership arrangement between the two companies, have been helping the Japanese company in other ways to get to grips with the slow-down in its primary markets. The business has too many products, unsustainable for the future. Its product line is being rationalized.

Equally interesting is the way Alex Trotman and the executive team at Ford itself are responding to the pressure to change. New car markets, particularly the vast potential of China, are firmly in Trotman's sights. Three things characterize Trotman's approach: the need to build a truly global, world-class organization; economies of scale and a relentless squeeze on costs; and, of course, quality. Ford has put $6 billion towards its world car programme, a global sourcing project of staggering proportions. This has meant the merger of its European and North American operations into a single unit, Ford Automotive Operations, and the creation of five vehicle centres (four in the US and one in Europe). The result – regional barriers are fast disappearing. Global sourcing has become the standard.

So the world is changing faster and faster, becoming the *CyberSociety* described by Steven Jones in his book of that name (1994), where the culture of computer and network-mediated communication changes much of what has gone before. 'On-line commerce' over the Internet, for example, is now a reality. Furthermore, it has been estimated that the total accumulation of scientific knowledge is doubling every ten years. The impact of this on society is dramatic: we see it perhaps most clearly in the business world. Tom Peters, in *Liberation Management* (1992), refers to it as the 'nanosecond nineties' and, suitably chastened by IBM and others' sudden fall from grace, he advocates shredding the old images of how businesses should do things. He's right, certainly about global change and probably about how businesses need to adapt. But a note of caution: some things don't change. We just don't understand them properly. Leadership is one of those things.

But let's deal with global change first.

The old order changeth, yielding place to new
Alfred, Lord Tennyson
(King Arthur in *Morte d'Arthur*)

Dragons and Sick Men

The General Agreement on Tariffs and Trade (GATT) reported in 1993 that there had been a shift in the rankings of the world's leading goods exporters. The US, Germany and Japan were in the top three. No surprises there. But Hong Kong had gained two places (eighth) and China was ninth. For commercial services exports there were no changes at the top either: the US was followed by France, Italy, Germany, Britain and Japan. Behind them, though, Singapore, South Korea, Hong Kong and Taiwan were all gaining ground in the top 20.

So what? Why should business leaders in the Western world do more than shrug?

In understanding this better we must bring the global picture into greater focus. The G7, the group of seven industrialized nations, have had a torrid time of it for a number of years now. Rich Thomas in *Newsweek*, for example, described the performance of the US as the 'best of a bad bunch' (18 July 1994, p 26). Since 1991, *Newsweek* declared, only the US has achieved solid growth (above 3 per cent a year), low inflation (less than 3 per cent) and created a substantial number of jobs (about 4.8 million). The rest of the G7 have struggled. What does this mean for the future? A new boom for the US? A resurgence of corporate America?

One look at the figures in Table 1.1 tells a fairly positive story about the outlook for growth in the G7 up to 2004. This is the view taken through a consensus survey of the leading forecasters in each of the G7 (*Consensus Economics*, April 1994). Of course, this is only a forecast (and economists *have* been known to be wrong). Perhaps US growth will be nearer 3 per cent. But it is certainly hard to see any of the G7, including the US, much exceeding these growth percentages.

Table 1.1 *Longer-term prospects: G7*

COUNTRY	Annual real GDP growth (% p.a.) 1996–2004	
Japan	3.2	
Canada	3.0	
Germany*	2.8	(2.2)
France	2.7	
US	2.7	
Italy	2.4	
UK	2.2	

*Total Germany; average growth rate for Western Germany only in brackets

Source: *Consensus Economics Survey* (April 1994)

The picture is fairly even across all seven. This is striking because Japan's prospects seem poor in relative terms, given the fantastic strength of its economy. More on this paradox in a page or two, for we need to dig down below the surface. For the moment let's just take the numbers. They are mesmerizing. Between 1990 and 1993 Japan amassed an accumulated current account surplus of around $360 billion. G7 and in particular US pressure on Tokyo to open the Japanese market more to imports through deregulation and income tax cuts has shrunk the surplus slightly but it is still on course to reach a staggering $1000 billion before the turn of the century, recent US threats of a trade war notwithstanding. For Western economies this is impressive indeed, but it is nothing new. There are, however, threats other than the economic imperialism of Japan.

Enter the Asian dragons – suddenly in the top 20 of goods and services exporters, remember. Hong Kong, Singapore, South Korea and Taiwan have taken giant-sized bites out of world GDP (gross domestic product), the share of visible exports and foreign exchange reserves, and will continue to do so. The graphs in Figures 1.1 and 1.2 say it all.

South Korea's GDP per head in 1962 was $110, the same as Sudan; by 1990 it was $6700 (*The Economist*, 30 October, 1993). China, Malaysia, Indonesia and Thailand are fast catching up.

Where Have all the Leaders Gone?

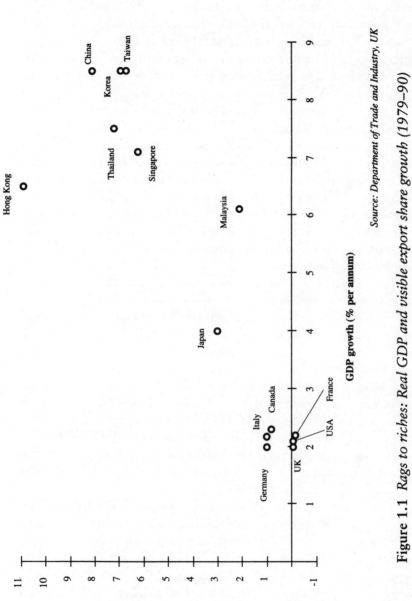

Figure 1.1 *Rags to riches: Real GDP and visible export share growth (1979–90)*

Source: Department of Trade and Industry, UK

25

Growth of 8 per cent and 9 per cent against 3 per cent for the best of the G7 is the reality. So too is the news that Beijing recently announced plans to create four internationally competitive vehicle manufacturers by 2010 which would rapidly make cars a part of Chinese family life. Those families, in China and the other increasingly affluent Asian societies, will want the houses, televisions, videos and refrigerators that most Westerners take for granted.

In the same issue *The Economist* makes a conservative estimate that the Asian market by 2000 will comprise some 1 billion consumers! This kind of 'sudden' entry to the world stage of eight East Asian fast-growing industrialized economies opens the door to exciting opportunities. More crucially, however, it poses considerable difficulties for Western businesses still locked into the mind-set of relatively stable markets and predictable competitive pressures, even factoring in the great impact Japan's gargantuan corporations have indirectly forced on the quality and efficiency of the West's industries.

'Yes, we all know we have to change!' comes the cry. 'Corporate transformation is the name of the game!'

Sure. But do we really appreciate the magnitude of the change? Or put another way: for the remainder of the 1990s how intense will these new competitive pressures become? To answer this requires a crystal ball. And the crystal ball in question is scenario planning. Coopers & Lybrand's Policy and Economics Group have extrapolated from a host of economic, social and political data to produce a long-term view of global economic prospects up to 2005 (Coopers & Lybrand, September 1993). Table 1.2 shows the optimistic and pessimistic scenarios and, more to the point, the broad assessment of whether the pessimistic or optimistic scenario is more probable.

The results are clear – or as clear as they can be when predicting the future. They suggest a continuing, steady relative decline of the US under the back-breaking burden of twin budget and trade deficits. American exports are reducing, the trade deficit widening. More importantly, there is a question mark over the sustained capacity of US firms to compete in global markets. Finally, the US share of world GDP is on a declining trend from about 23 per cent currently projected to 18 per cent by 2010.

This time, however, it isn't Japan pouncing predator-like on US weakness. Still immensely strong in the mid-1990s, by 2005 it may well be running out of steam. Could Japan eventually be

Table 1.2 *Dragons and sick men ... 2005*

Country/region	Optimistic scenario	Pessimistic scenario	Assessment
US	• Steady growth at over 3% p.a	• Continued relative decline (growth below 2% p.a)	• Pessimistic
Japan	• Continued rapid growth (4%+ p.a)	• Decelerating (growth only 2% p.a)	• Pessimistic/unclear
Western Europe	• Growth above 3% p.a. • Unemployment falls	• Slow growth (1–2% p.a) • Unemployment rate rises towards 20%	• Pessimistic
Eastern Europe/ CIS	• Rapid growth in Eastern Europe • Stability in Russia	• Little growth in Eastern Europe • Chaos in Russia	• Unclear
China	• Rapid growth of 1980s sustained • Economic reforms continue	• Overheating forces sharp growth slowdown • Economic reforms reversed	• Optimistic/unclear
Asian dragons	• 7% growth sustained	• Growth slows markedly	• Optimistic

dubbed the 'sick man' of the Asia-Pacific? The idea is not so startling. There have been bankruptcies among Japanese companies at the rate of around 1000 per month for the past two years and, even worse, Japan's 150 banks have suffered an average 30 per cent decline in profits for five years running. Only the largest 10 or 11 commercial banks have sufficiently recovered their capital ratio to go hunting abroad, particularly in Asia. Even so, the danger is that they will sooner or later risk massive exposure in places like China, repeating the lending disasters in Latin America in the 1970s. Equally, the practice of lifetime employment, to which the top 300 or 400 Japanese companies staunchly adhere, may well become a terrible drain on competitive strength; there are stark parallels with the commitment to providing lifetime employment to employees of the German steel giant Krupp, a commitment that brought the business to the verge of collapse after a century of success. More fundamental for future governments is the rapidly ageing population; as more and more Japanese reach retirement and therefore pay no income tax, so Japan's consumption tax will have to be raised in leaps and bounds to make up the shortfall. Worse yet, its future generation of workers, the youth of Japan or *shinjinrui* – new human race – identify less and less with their 'workaholic' parents, demanding much more than a lifetime commitment to the corporate colossi of Japanese industry. Political upheaval, the erosion of the corporatist work ethic and cultural homogeneity by individualism, and being outperformed every year by the Asian dragons as well as China and even India: it is some way off, perhaps, but in the shadow of the mountain of its trade surplus the ultimate seeds of Japan's demise are already apparent.

On the other side of the world Europe and Britain are recovering from recession and without the huge size (and attendant risks) of Japan and America's economies, their prospects might be moderately good. Germany and its neighbours have on their doorstep the growing economies of Poland, Hungary and the Czech and Slovak republics to boost trade. Nonetheless, in the final analysis unemployment across Europe is likely seriously to hobble economic performance.

Meanwhile countries in Eastern Europe, as well as Russia and the emerging nations around it, may well be confounded by ethnic, political and economic chaos until well beyond 2005. Trouble in the rebel Russian republic of Chechnya may be a signpost to the future.

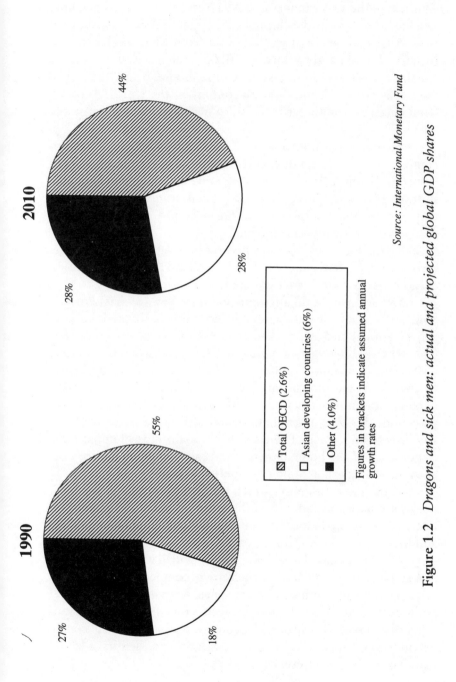

2010

44%

28%

28%

1990

55%

27%

18%

☒ Total OECD (2.6%)

☐ Asian developing countries (6%)

■ Other (4.0%)

Figures in brackets indicate assumed annual growth rates

Source: International Monetary Fund

Figure 1.2 *Dragons and sick men: actual and projected global GDP shares*

This leaves the real winners in Eastern and Southern Asia. China and the other rapidly developing economies of Asia-Pacific are set to increase their share of world output from what was less than a fifth in 1990 to nearly a third by 2010, as the pie-charts in Figure 1.2 show. Even more impressive, China should, by 2010, achieve the status as the second largest economy in the world. And it is from here that the threat to Western businesses will increasingly come.

Of course, this is not to say that competition between Western companies is any less, nor that the Japanese juggernaut is a spent force. Far from it. But the growing wave of trade liberalization, shifting economic power and additional competitive pressures will add to the complexity of business life and thus to the complexity of business leadership.

Will your business be swamped by innovative, leading-edge, zero-defect, perfect quality products and services from the Asian dragons and a dozen other competitive nations? Yes.

Can your business do anything about it? Yes. Michael Porter's bold analysis of the fundamental determinants of national and organizational success, packed into 800 pages of his book, *The Competitive Advantage of Nations* (1990), leads to a few simple, but vitally important conclusions. 'What I have found,' he writes, 'is that firms will not ultimately succeed unless they base their strategies on improvement and innovation, a willingness to compete, and a realistic understanding of their national environment and how to improve it. The view that globalization eliminates the importance of the home base rests on false premises, as does the alluring strategy of avoiding competition' (p30).

The answers aren't easy, which goes without saying. Big businesses are hard to change, and there are no guarantees. But with risk comes opportunity. On the one hand countries like China and Indonesia are worrying threats. On the other hand, their low wage economies have large, increasingly skilled workforces which global businesses can use to their own competitive advantage. Seizing these opportunities can, at times, seem both daunting and perilous. But we can all think of projects, companies, corporations – any of a thousand human endeavours – that have been successful beyond expectation. And in most cases we can identify a leader who has made the difference.

Cathedral, Printing Press or Information Superhighway?

Up until the Middle Ages, architecture was the great script of the world. Ideas, religious, social or philosophical, were perpetuated from one generation to another in the stone of buildings and monuments. A book in those far-off days, crafted and illuminated by scholars, was a fragile thing, the ideas within it living only in the minds of the very few who read it and enduring only as long as the book itself. But everything changed in the fifteenth century. Gutenberg invented the printing press.

In *Notre Dame de Paris* Victor Hugo described this as 'the greatest event in history ... the mother of revolutions.' Why? Because you can destroy a great edifice and thus the ideas it represents, but you cannot expunge ideas in printed form, scattered on the winds and ubiquitous. In the Middle Ages this was indeed a revolution. The construction of the magnificent cathedrals of Europe, so long the dominant expression of all that was European civilization, began to decline. With that decline came an explosion of thought endlessly pumped out by the printing press and presaging the enormous social, religious and political upheavals of Europe and then the world.

This was, in its way, the first information revolution. What we are witnessing now in the nanosecond 1990s is the extension of this revolution. We call it the global market and the information superhighway. Victor Hugo called it:

> ... a construction which grows and mounts in spirals without end; here is a confusion of tongues, ceaseless activity, indefatigable labour, fierce rivalry between all of mankind...

Indeed our world has changed, and in many respects we recognize these changes as beyond the capacity of the old, huge corporations to adapt sufficiently fast. Change is happening now. We are in the midst of revolution. The only way to adapt and survive is to stand outside it, to see the global changes with as much of the same perspective as history granted Victor Hugo. This is one of the challenges of leadership.

$$\boxed{2}$$

EXTRAORDINARY TIMES, EXTRAORDINARY CHALLENGES

Into Orbit

On 25 May 1961 John F Kennedy spoke to a joint session of the US Congress. In words that are now famous he said:

> ... I believe that this nation should commit itself to achieving the goal, before this decade is out, of landing a man on the moon and returning him safely to earth. No single space project in this period will be more impressive to mankind, or more important for the long-range exploration of space; and none will be so difficult or expensive to accomplish ...

In 1969 Neil Armstrong walked on the moon.

What had got him there? Was it leadership?

I debated this point with a group of executives over dinner one evening. Most of them, tough-minded cynics that they were, argued that it wasn't. 'The Cold War was the reason for the space race and the moon landings,' said one dismissively.

I was not so sure. The Cold War was the context, just as Hitler's imperialism in Europe was the context of the late 1930s. Then, Neville Chamberlain was unable to rise to the occasion and simply pandered to Hitler, claiming 'peace in our time' on the basis of what soon turned out to be a worthless piece of paper. In 1961, pride dented by the accomplishments of the Soviet Union in putting Yuri Gagarin into orbit around Earth, the US was on the back foot. Was the space race inevitable? Given the circumstances of the Cold War, perhaps it was. But by itself the Cold War could not have produced the preparedness to commit such vast resources and energy, nor engendered the enormous collective will that brought men to the Moon.

The Cold War didn't. Leadership did.

An Articulate Voice

Yes, truly, it is a great thing for a Nation that it get an articulate voice; that it produce a man who will speak-forth melodiously what the heart of it means!

Thomas Carlyle
(*On Heroes, Hero-Worship, and the Heroic in History*, Lecture III, 1840)

Everyone Has a Theory

One of Kennedy's campaigners, James McGregor Burns, referred to leadership as 'one of the most observed and least understood phenomena on earth.' In other words, everyone has a theory. As I intimated at the start of this chapter, discussions on leadership often generate considerable heat, not least because people disagree on whether Ms X or Mr Y are actually leaders. This is particularly noticeable in the gap between the Anglo-Saxon (British, American, etc) and the European and Japanese view of the business world. Leaders are placed in an entirely different category from managers in both the US and Britain. In those countries leaders are believed to have the individual power to change a company's fortunes, whereas in Germany or the Netherlands a much more collegiate style of *management* pertains. The German concepts of *mitbestimung* (co-determination) and *Vorstand* (management board) are generally more important than an individual's leadership. In Japan, consensus decision-making is overlaid by the *sempai–kohai* (superior–subordinate) relationship inherited from Japan's long feudal age, making leadership largely a function of status and rank.

These cultural differences can have real and quite dramatic implications. Consider Reed Elsevier, the international publishing group with over $4 billion turnover and 25,000 employees. When Reed International of the UK and Elsevier of the Netherlands merged in 1993, much was made of the similarities between the two organizations, the close business associations between the two countries and the successful historical precedents of Royal Dutch Shell and Unilever. By June 1994 one of the co-chairmen, Peter Davis, had resigned. The reason? Dutch management practice emphasizes collaborative and collegiate direction at the top. Peter Davis' style was typically Anglo-Saxon: a strong chief executive running the business himself. Proposed reallocation of responsibilities within the executive committee would have left strategy, management development and corporate communications to the co-chairs. For Peter Davis this was unacceptable.

It is no surprise then that much of the literature on leadership is American and British. Theory, research, conventional wisdom – all have much to say on leadership. All can be reduced to a number of broad themes.

- *Born to lead:* leaders are born, not made. The Ancients believed this. Greek and Roman history is filled with characters who rose to fame or infamy because they apparently were born to it. The idea has considerable force; think how often you have had conversations which included a comment from someone that so-and-so 'is a born leader'. Usually this is a convenient mask for the real explanation; that some leaders perform with such ease and accomplishment that it seems ridiculous to suggest they learned these skills.
- *Universal traits:* if leadership isn't in-born, then what are the physical, mental and personality traits that produce it? Up to the 1950s serious research failed to clear the muddy waters. It had only delivered endless lists of traits which, much like astrological 'profiles', can be used to describe anyone and give the appearance of explanation without explaining anything at all. 'Tactful, intelligent, persuasive, dominant, extroverted, ambitious, motivated, aggressive', and so on. So what? Millions of people have these qualities. We are still left with the question, 'What makes a leader?' The most that can be said for Trait Theory is that it has identified that successful leaders generally have higher intelligence than their followers. Of course, this is by no means a universal rule.
- *Depends on the situation:* if traits don't help, then perhaps we should be looking outwards rather than inwards. How does the situation affect leadership and followers' performance and satisfaction? At the head of this line of enquiry was Fred

Fiedler whose research seemed to show that leadership effectiveness was influenced by the favourableness of a situation combined with the leadership style. He identified three critical factors:

- leader–member relationship (the extent to which leaders are accepted by their followers);
- task structure (how tightly defined the work is); and
- position power (formal authority invested in the job-role).

Fiedler discovered that the uncompromising, directive leader was most effective, as you might expect, when the situation was highly unfavourable (for example, when followers don't accept their leader, the work is ill-defined and formal authority is not attributed to the leader's position). When the going gets tough the tough are the best leaders to get going. However, the same applies in highly favourable situations, too. Odd, to say the least. But perhaps not. Fiedler explained that when leaders have full authority, informal backing from their team and a well-structured task, followers are not only ready to be directed but expect to be told what to do. By contrast, in the intermediate range of favourableness (situations that are neither too good nor too bad), a more lenient, person-oriented style is the most effective leadership style.

- *Do it with style*: research has gone further with Fiedler's basic concepts into specifying the main types or styles of leadership. Blake and Mouton's managerial grid, Reddin's 3D model of leadership effectiveness, and Rensis Likert's systems approach are all well-known and widely used style models. They emphasize styles such as:
  - autocratic and exploitative;
  - directive and task-focused;
  - supportive and relationship-oriented; and
  - democratic, participative and empowering.

  Some are said to be better than others and indeed work better from situation to situation. Of course, while these theories help individuals to understand how they typically lead, they also (impossibly) expect managers to learn to switch styles according to need.

- *Action-centred leadership*: in Britain John Adair has developed his ideas on working groups, organizations and leadership, initially from observations at the Royal Military Academy at Sandhurst, to pinpoint three overlapping elements (task, team and individual). Problems in one element

35

affect the others. He describes leadership as providing direction, inspiring others, creating teams and generating acceptance from followers.

The leadership concept is encapsulated within the action-
centred learning model, which provides a route for leadership
training. However, Adair's theory leans heavily on Abraham
Maslow's hierarchy of needs and Henri Fayol's theories and
techniques of management, both conceived at a time (the
1950s and early 1900s respectively) when business and organizational life could not have anticipated the global, informa-
tion-age 1990s.

● *Become yourself:* Warren Bennis is probably the most famous
of the leadership thinkers. Professor of management at the
University of Southern California, Bennis, together with Burt
Nanus, has argued that the best leaders are ideas people and
that becoming a leader requires self-fulfilment, knowing and
becoming yourself. Leaders then are characterized by four key
abilities:

- the management of attention (creating a compelling vision);
- the management of meaning (communicating vision to
  produce action);
- the management of trust (which demands constancy); and
- the management of self (self-understanding, resilience,
  persistence).

Bennis has made a significant contribution to leadership
theory but the notion of self-fulfilment as the key to becoming
a leader is a trifle hard to swallow.

No More Presidential Leaders...

There is a crisis of presidential leadership in the United States.
Opinion polls mark Bill Clinton as one of the most unpopular
presidents ever. Even his successes have been overshadowed
by deep and widespread misgivings. For instance, the resolution of the Haiti problem in 1994 represented an excellent
opportunity for Clinton to win back admiration and support,
yet a *CNN/USA Today/Gallup* poll found that only 15 per cent
of Americans credited Clinton with the deal (70 per cent said
Jimmy Carter deserved most credit).

Little wonder then that the Democrats suffered the worst mid-term election reverses in November 1994 in 50 years. The US electorate had asked for widespread policy changes and got, instead, dithering and drift. They punished the President and the party holding most of the power.

But why is this a crisis?

In 1978 *Business Week* (11 September) argued that Congress was grabbing more and more power away from the President's office as a direct result of the poor leadership abilities of the presidents. First there is the War Powers Act, which shifts approval to Congress for armed action ordered by the President. Next there is the Budget and Impoundment Control Act which enables Congress, effectively against the President's will, to force through appropriations which it has itself authorized.

In short, the problem is older than the last few years. Moreover, as the nation expects more and more of its presidents, so its political machinery cuts away more and more of their power.

What is Leadership?

The development of leadership theory has floundered somewhat. Of course, looking at the immense volumes of so-called leadership training on offer in every corner of the globe would prompt you to think the opposite. Still, I think every manager who ever goes near a leadership training course (even big ticket programmes at the best business schools) comes away wondering whether the knowledge acquired really has equipped him or her with what it takes to be a leader.

The more empirical research that is done makes a lie of the generalized theories of management taught worldwide in business schools. Management is complex, fragmented, its activities brief, opportunistic, predominantly verbal; leadership more so. Management reacts. Leadership transforms. It makes a difference. To get to grips with what leadership is we need to look at it not simply in terms of the characteristics and actions of the individual, but with reference to what Czarniawska-Joerges and Wolff (1991) have called 'the political, social and economic context of organizing' (p 542). This does not mean that leadership depends on the situation. It means that it is part of the wider environment of business. It is both substantive and symbolic, and it is more than Rosabeth Moss Kanter's 'vision thing'.

A perspective as broad as this one is a fine thing, but it's hard to tie down to specifics without concrete examples. A good starting point is to look back at President Kennedy, specifically his speech to Congress on 25 May 1961, when he asked the American people to commit to the extraordinary venture of landing a man on the moon.

Of course, delivering speeches is not leadership, but the entire text of Kennedy's speech provides an excellent record of what leadership is and how it works, summarized as the leadership domain in Figure 2.1. There is the *context* – what JFK describes as 'extraordinary times'. There is the *risk*, both of failure and inaction. There is *unpredictability*, the capacity to surprise the audience and the nation with the ambition and breathtaking extent of the programme. There is the *conviction* that it is the right thing to do. And finally there is the creation of a *critical mass* sufficient to launch and sustain the whole enormous enterprise.

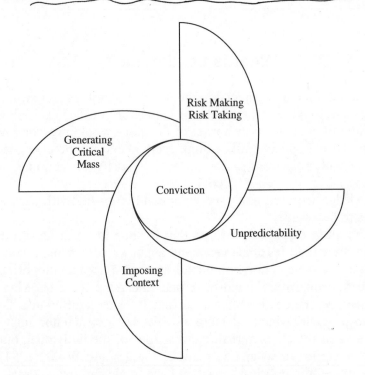

Figure 2.1 *The leadership domain*

Ａnalysᵇ Context

These are extraordinary times. And we face an extraordinary
challenge. Our strength as well as our convictions have imposed
upon this nation the role of leader in freedom's cause.

So begins the speech. The immediacy with which Kennedy sets
the context is striking. Although the full speech ranges across
economic and social progress in the US, defence, intelligence,
disarmament and space, the context he emphasizes is the commitment to freedom and the United States' role in history. Moreover,
he states clearly at the outset that the context itself is not ordinary
and, by implication, that his expectations of both himself and his
nation cannot be ordinary either. This is where people begin to
understand that they can rise beyond the humdrum of life and
achieve far more than they ever believed possible.

Other writers might call this vision, but the word 'vision' misses
the point. It has come to imply strategy, long-range plans,
superordinate goals. But when leaders create context, they articulate for individuals their place and role in an enterprise both in
striving for a future goal and in knowing what it means. To know
what it means is to understand, at an intellectual and an emotional
level, where your enterprise itself stands in relation to the world,
in the past, now and in the future.

It is true to say that it is when the world around us is at its most
humdrum or its most confusing that we yearn for leadership to
give clarity to this context.

Risk

... while we cannot guarantee that we shall one day be first, we can
guarantee that any failure to make this effort will make us last. We
face an additional risk by making it in full view of the world, but
... this very risk enhances our stature when we are successful.

This is the making of risk, the creation of opportunity. Risk
making and risk taking are dangerous. Risks of the magnitude JFK
was outlining have been diminished by time. People have walked
on the Moon. Unmanned probes have explored Mars, Venus,
Saturn, Jupiter and beyond. Satellites are an everyday part of life.
Indeed our day-to-day communications and entertainment depend
on them. Organizations like CNN could not have existed otherwise.

We take this technology for granted. In 1961, when Kennedy made his speech, the most the US had achieved was Alan Shepard's 15 minute 22 second sub-orbital space-flight – disparagingly dubbed a 'flea-hop'. It is only with a wrench that we realize how great was the risk attendant on an idea to take people to the moon *for the first time*.

Making the risk public is even more dangerous, particularly for politicians or anyone in the public eye. Explaining risk to people can lead to disaster. Like a grenade, it can go off in your face. Knowledge of risk can bring fear, and fear paralysis. Using it to your advantage, to sweep aside reservations and active resistance and to mobilize effort takes skill. Managers control risk; leaders take risks. Threat and fear of failure then become catalysts for action, challenges to which individuals aspire.

Unpredictability

Since early in my term, our efforts in space have been under review .... Now it is time to take longer strides – time for a great new American enterprise – time for this nation to take a clearly leading role in space achievement, which in many ways may hold the key to our future on earth.

Going beyond the norm, challenging the status quo always, of its very nature, requires unpredictability. Managers are part of the pattern, leaders move outside it. They change the pattern, both inside their firms and outside, in their markets.

In Britain in 1970 an official of the Transport and General Workers Union (TGWU) remarked, 'Democracy is not something that happens naturally in organizations – bureaucracy is.' Big organizations are fat and sluggish – most of them anyway. Even the best (IBM once) fail because inertia becomes all-pervasive. What we must remember is the obvious, that organizations are made up of people and people become sluggish, bored, and lose their edge.

It is the unpredictable quality of leadership that grabs attention, that turns heads from the constantly competing demands of the here-and-now and the dangers of navel-gazing. Some business leaders emphasize this quality above others. Ricardo Semler, chief executive of the Brazilian company Semco, threw out all the rules when he took over. 'Semco's standard policy is no policy,' he declares in his book *Maverick!*, the title of which says it all.

Conviction

> If we are to go only half way, or reduce our sights in the face of
> difficulty, in my judgment it would be better not to go at all.

Kennedy's message is unequivocal. Despite saying in his very next
sentence, 'Now this is a choice which this country must make,'
his own conviction is plain. He is *leading* the nation. Later he
declares: 'I believe we should go to the moon.'

Friedrich Nietzsche, the nineteenth century German philoso-
pher, observed: 'Men believe in the truth of all that is seen to be
strongly believed in.' It matters not that the truth is vile: Hitler
was the adored leader of a nation which believed fervently in his
'truths'. What counts is conviction. We will not follow people
who lack belief in themselves and their goals.

One of the causes of the current malaise in Western politics is
this obvious fact. The electorates see through the veil of political
oratory to what lies behind: short-term political survival, maintenance of the status quo, protection of self-interest. Western
nations lack purpose and there are no leaders to believe in.

A few years ago I was discussing major change programmes
with the chief executive of a large London-based company. At one
point he said to me (only half-jokingly): 'My philosophy about
change is straightforward: I'm the boss. I'm right. This is my view
and this is what we're going to do.'

I think that puts the case for conviction quite well.

Critical Mass

> ... in a very real sense, it will not be one man going to the moon –
> if we make this judgment affirmatively, it will be an entire nation.
> For all of us must work to put him there.

Neil Armstrong would not have walked on the moon if the whole
project had not received sufficient impetus. All of us, at some time
in our business lives, have been part of an initiative which seemed,
at the outset, to have the hallmarks of success, but never quite
made it. Organizations are littered with the bones of 'change
programmes', many with state-of-the-art project management
controls and endless resources, that collapsed before they got into
their stride. We've all heard the moaned refrain, 'If only it had
been led from the top!'

Leaders ensure that energy is released, that it is sustained across any number of initiatives, as well as ensuring that people in the day-to-day operation of the business get it right every day. That's hard to do. Generating the energy for all this takes personal energy, skill and judgement. What are the priorities? Where to drive most of my effort? How much resource can we divert from other important activities? How much can the organization take?

Everything Else is Management

One of the inevitable risks of trying to define something as complex and elusive as leadership is that you open yourself to the criticism (not least from business leaders themselves) that you've left something out. Part of the difficulty lies in identifying where management ends and leadership begins. And it is precisely at this point (wherever that is) that a large gulf opens up. Most leaders, even when they recognize they've leapt the dizzying heights, can't articulate what's on the other side, at least not very readily. That applies to the successful business leaders interviewed for this book as well as the many others I have had the good fortune to meet. Most leaders don't spend their time in self-analysis.

Most managers, with or without self-analysis, never cross the gulf. I have no truck with organizations which claim that *everyone* in them is a leader. The vast majority of staff and managers do not lead; call them leaders if you like, but don't expect them to lead. They won't. They can't. Indeed many are not even allowed to – organizational bureaucracy is designed to prevent it. Even those organizations whose innards have not ossified constrain individuals (often rightly so) to specific roles where, at best, people manage creatively but are never leaders. An organization filled with leaders would be a brawl.

This does not mean that leadership cannot be developed, but it is difficult. If it were easy there would not be (literally) tens of thousands of training courses worldwide devoted to the topic. Apart from the obvious fact that *training* leadership does not work, the subject matter of 'leadership training' is generally far off the mark. It makes simple, often specious assumptions about complex human behaviour.

This does not mean that only senior figures in organizations are leaders. We all know instances of bad bosses managing good leaders. We also know that effective leaders can make a big difference to small units in a larger business. I hypothesize that the success (measured on profitability and a range of other performance indicators) of individual business units or profit centres in a large corporation is consistently linked to the personal effectiveness (leadership) of the business unit or profit centre manager. This is not to say that leadership is just a more effective form of management; the two are different. Leaders *do* different things, as we shall shortly see.

In any event, if we are ever to understand leadership better and gain leverage off it, then we must not pretend that everyone is a leader, or that leadership can be 'taught' in a two-week training course. This is because it is not simply about developing a specific skill-set. Leadership relies heavily on the combination of skills, both managerial skills and other qualities, and their balance. This book is an attempt to dissect leadership and define, not skills or competencies, but the broad patterns of behaviour that enable leadership to work, to produce complex outputs that have a significant impact on people's performance and the performance of the organization. Some of these patterns of leadership behaviour run counter to 'good management': they are the kinds of things that organizations, typically run with an eye to control and not to risk and opportunism, rarely reward or actively develop and almost invariably suppress. Organizations (and the people who inhabit them) always have needed and always will need some form of stability, and although the world is changing faster than ever and we need to be flexible, to change, we also need to be stable while we do it. This is the dilemma organizations face and ironically it is leaders who face the task of not only resolving but capitalizing on the dilemma.

The Age of Leisure, much-vaunted in the 1960s as the just inheritance of the Western world's amazing technological and industrial advances, has never materialized. People work harder now than ever before. Managers in particular have discovered that it is not enough to be a manager: hi-tech companies require hi-tech competence in addition to management competence. Yet despite 60 hour working weeks and enormous efforts in business education (25 per cent of all US undergraduates, some 240,000 a year, are majoring in business studies), the greater proportion of these managers return average, not to say indifferent, performance in their businesses.

Some, however, produce startlingly good results, year after year. Some capture market niches the rest of the world didn't know were there. Some turn dying corporations around. Some sustain organizations against all the odds. In short, some make a difference. These are the business leaders and they share some, more rarely all, of the following patterns of behaviour in the leadership domain:

- imposing *context* in an enterprise and for the people in it;
- making *risks* and taking *risks*;
- creating *unpredictability* in themselves, the enterprise and its markets;
- sustaining *conviction*; and
- generating *critical mass*.

What Price Leadership?

Industry Week in 1991 (15 April) reported a survey describing executive pay as 'sickening, infuriating, disgraceful'. Strong stuff – and it seems justified. *Business Week*'s special report (25 April, 1994) on their 44th annual Executive Pay Scorecard (covering 361 companies) began with the exasperated title: 'That eye-popping executive pay: Is anybody worth this much?'. Chairman of Walt Disney Co., Michael Eisner, raked in $203,010,590 in 1993! Eye-popping, indeed. He's a fair way ahead, but he's not alone. The Pay Scorecard lists the highest paid executives (in thousands of dollars):

	1993 salary	Long-term compensation	Total Pay
Michael D Eisner Walt Disney	$750	$202,261	$203,011
Sanford I Weill Travelers	$4,291	$48,519	$52,810
Joseph R Hyde III Autozone	$1,103	$31,117	$32,220
Charles N Mathewson International Game Technology	$628	$21,603	$22,231
Alan C Greenberg Bear Stearns	$11,988	$3,927	$15,915
N Wayne Huizenga Blockbuster Entertainment	$557	$15,000	$15,557

Is executive pay out of control? Most articles on the matter start (and end) with the question, 'Is anyone worth that much?'. In fact the whole issue has gone so far as to receive treatment in an academic study by Mitchell, George-Falvy and Crandall (1993) who suggest that the obvious inequity between the pay of business leaders and most corporate employees could lead to serious difficulties of low morale and destructive behaviour. Even President Clinton got in on the act in 1993, putting a $1 million cap on executive pay that is deductible. What did the corporations do? Paid the higher taxes, of course. Many even raised pay, treating the $1 million cap as a minimum.

What's going on?

The thrust of the critics seems to be around justice and fairness. The concern of the corporations seems entirely at odds with this. Moreover, effort, skill and performance of CEOs are not always (ever?) crucial either. Executives frequently get annual pay rises despite patchy performance and lagging shareholder returns. Why? Because leadership counts. More so than ever before. The comfort of having a leader in place who is known (as long as the business's performance isn't too bad) is worth big money. Think of any of the six organizations above abruptly losing its 'leader'...

That, at least, is how the stock market values leadership.

3

IMPOSING CONTEXT

A Vision for Big Blue

When Lou Gerstner left RJR Nabisco to take on the top job at IBM in March 1993 he came with a track record of having achieved dramatic turnaround and growth in the loss-making Travel Related Services (TRS) division of American Express. Between 1978 and 1987 TRS net income increased some 500 per cent. With that background it was no wonder that expectations skyrocketed that Gerstner would produce a 'vision' for the troubled Big Blue. After all that's what leaders do, don't they?

Gerstner's response was widely reported in the business media. He said:

> There has been a lot of speculation that I'm going to deliver a 'vision' of the future of IBM. The last thing IBM needs right now is a vision. What IBM needs right now is a series of very tough-minded, market-driven and highly effective strategies that deliver performance in the market place and shareholder value.

Slavish adherence to the notion that organizations need a vision and chief executives must provide it is where we are today in the mid-1990s. Vision has become a fad, and there are times when visions are only for prophets, not for business leaders. What Gerstner was doing was setting the context, ensuring that not only employees but customers, suppliers and the stock market understood clearly where IBM was and what it had to do, *now*, *next week*, not in five years. 'In his early days at IBM,' writes Paul Carroll in *Big Blues* (1993), his riveting analysis of IBM's catastrophic decline:

> Gerstner took some decisive, positive steps. He effectively abolished the Management Committee, saying that he didn't believe in

rule by committee. Gerstner also tried to forbid anyone from making a presentation to him using foils. For a while, executives didn't know what to do. They could barely speak without their foils. But Gerstner insisted that if someone had something to say, he should just say it. Gerstner, in general, dispensed with the formalities of IBM meetings. He typically blew into a meeting room after everyone was assembled and, without any pleasantries, got started. He asked quick, tough, almost rude questions. Then he wound things up in perhaps fifteen minutes. (p.353)

Arresting IBM's decline will not be easy but Gerstner has made the right start, including a dramatic shift in strategy with a $3.3 billion hostile takeover bid of the software house Lotus Development Corporation – the biggest software takeover bid to date.

It is too easy (for chief executives as well as everyone else) to fly off into the stratosphere in pursuit of grand visions or become sunk in the morass of day-to-day finance, marketing, operations, and budgets and thus never see the wood for the trees or, just as damagingly, drift into the routine of formulaic strategic planning that accepts the business as it is, its competitors as unchanged, its markets as fixed and its options as more of the same.

Imposing context is concerned with integrating these things, rather than planning strategy and grappling with the future. It is a leader's way of providing purpose over and above the buzz of organizational activity, of concentrating attention by cutting through the noisy stream of conflicting information, of conveying proportion when the allure of short-term success or the wretchedness of setback and failure threaten to undermine a firm's accomplishments and objectives. It is a way of interpreting the world for employees, of saying what matters and what does not.

It is a mistake to look too far ahead. Only one link in
the chain of destiny can be handled at a time.

Winston Churchill

Out of Synch

Setting the context can be tough for both leaders and their organizations. Peter Sherlock, Chief Executive of the UK firm NFC, formerly the National Freight Consortium, left in 1994 after 18 months for reasons that some analysts ascribed to his aggressive management style and others put down to the refusal of the organization's old guard to accept the upheaval and pace of change Peter Sherlock was driving.

The UK freight industry is in crisis. As more and more companies contract out and customers demand greater value for money, the larger operators like NFC are forced into more direct competition with newer, faster competitors whose cost bases are lower. Sherlock had made it clear that wide-ranging cost-cutting and management changes would have to be driven through fast. NFC, an employee co-operative with a culture of traditional values, was out of synch with its chief executive.

The Vision Thing

There have been few real attempts to understand 'vision'. It has been popularly credited with being vital to setting organizational direction and in providing a kind of filtering role in a management team's setting of strategic plans. However, so faddish has the idea become that leadership and vision are now constant companions, rarely seen out by themselves.

The media tell us every leader should have one, including presidents and prime ministers. Organizations, we are assured, will be lost without one. An image of the future will be a beacon for the organization; it will help to steer it through the dangerous reefs and shallows of global competition; it will somehow secure the future...

I am not so sure about this vision thing. We need to understand better what vision is and when it is appropriate. Westley and Mintzberg (1989) take us some of the way there. They propose four aspects that seem to have something to do with vision:

- visionary style: for example, percipience, a capacity to anticipate what may be important in the future;
- strategic process: procedural methods, deliberative or sudden;
- strategic content: what to believe in, how the business is organized, what the product or service is; and
- external context: the market, the target size of the business, and so forth.

But where does vision come from and why does it matter? There is no doubt that leaders construct a view of the future of the organization from their own experiences and beliefs.

Personality may be important in this regard – you will behave in particular ways, value certain options over others, prefer one course of action and dismiss another because of your personality type – but personality influences are often over-blown. By contrast, organizational and market conditions will strongly influence a leader's vision by generating new possibilities and closing down others, thereby shifting the vision onto new or alterative routes. True enough, but I am convinced that vision in great leaders is also about their capacity to avoid foreclosure, to refuse to accept organizational and market conditions as they are, to step outside the box and *make a vision work despite the odds*. To a great extent this comes down to risk and I deal with it in more detail in the next chapter.

Let us not, however, be seduced into blindly accepting first that we know what vision really is, and second, that the only type of vision that matters is action-oriented, risk-embracing, long-term and inspirational. Are these characteristics right for every organization and every situation? My answer is a resounding no. Laurie Larwood, Mark Kriger and Cecilia Falbe, in their 1993 analysis of vision – perhaps the first systematic study of the phenomenon – sound a cautionary note in this regard, arguing that 'although sometimes romanticized in the popular press, [it] may not be suitable to all situations' (p 234). A live example of this is Lou Gerstner's comments on vision at IBM, mentioned at the start of this chapter.

I believe that 'vision' is misleading on its own. Like many popular management ideas it has been absorbed unquestioningly – not to say unthinkingly – into the business psyche. To set about producing and then sticking to a long-term vision, simply because everyone else does this, is more common than you might believe. Managers can be very much like sheep: witness the annual round of fads, uncritically endorsed by many managers and trundled into their firms as the latest panacea. We need to be asking what the vision is for, who it is aimed at (customers, stockholders or employees?) and, indeed, whether it is not just a distraction from the things that matter now. Much better for leaders to understand that vision, in some circumstances, is not important and that, when it is, it is only one part of the requirement on leaders to impose context.

Interpreting the World to Concentrate Attention

Sensitivity to the organization's culture, as well as its markets, business priorities and operational requirements, is vital. Leaders recognize not only the critical moments of challenge and opportunity upon which an organization's success may hinge but also the true nature of the constraints under which they operate. They understand the strengths and weaknesses of their business. That means access to information, *lots* of information. Nelson Robertson of General Accident says candidly:

> I'm a great believer in getting information and advice from as many sources as possible. That includes, obviously, the people who report to me directly as well as at least two layers down. But I also believe in using consultants – the external, up-to-date view on a particular issue is crucial. Put all this together and you still make the decision yourself, but it's a better decision.

'I have in place what I call an early warning system,' says Alex Watson, President and CEO of Chep in Europe, 'an external network which enables me to better understand the moves in the market over the coming months and years. But this is becoming much more complex, dealing with global business.... I think it is essential for organizations to touch all the corners of the business community: in the past Chep didn't do this – it was too insular and monopolistic. Things are different now. I meet people all over Europe – customers, people inside and outside the market and this business.'

Derek Wanless, Group Chief Executive at NatWest Group, puts it another way: 'My personal style is to analyse issues out, to ask questions of detail, to get views on the table. It's not the quickest way of doing things, but in a group of this size and diversity I can't know everything about every business and its market. I'm much more about testing people out so that we have as much information as possible.' Certainly this was important when Wanless took on the top job at NatWest three years ago, at a time when the British banking industry as a whole had got itself into a mess with poor lending, but also, as Wanless points out, because of 'what had gone wrong in strategy formulation'.

'I decided,' continues Wanless, 'that we had to force *ourselves* as a team – rather than relying on consultants – to thoroughly analyse the business in all of its markets. There were really just two questions we wanted to answer in each case: firstly, how attractive is the market?; secondly, how much does NatWest need to change to win in that market?'

The result was a fairly simple two-dimensional matrix through which the senior team could make decisions on maintenance, growth, divestment and so on, but more importantly for what those decisions told Wanless about what NatWest Group would look like. Would the businesses be coherent as a group? The process of imposing context in a large organization is partly about attaining coherence – both real and perceived. Otherwise there is a very real danger that, at worst, the individual businesses (and the individuals in them) will be pulling in entirely different directions or, at best, there will be little or no value added by the group structure. 'Synergy,' declares Wanless with a smile, 'equals zero until proved otherwise.'

The leader's role in understanding the world, often from a different perspective, and therefore concentrating organizational attention on what matters is given a different slant by Alex Trotman at Ford. As outlined in Chapter 1 he is in the process of driving through massive changes in the way the company operates. At the heart of it is his intention to build a global, world-class organization. What that means in practice is that the old region-ally-based structure (reasonably successful for 90 years, remember) which engenders what Trotman calls 'regional thinking and regional action' has got to be replaced by a truly global operation. The old way, he insists, 'is not going to work in the next century. The winners of the next century will not think or act that way.' Part of his role in this is to be 'a messenger from the past'. He goes on to say:

> I think we've learned many lessons from the formation of Ford of Europe in 1967. I think we can learn a heck of a lot from the mistakes we've made over the last twenty or thirty years … . I've played a major role in interpreting those mistakes.

Likewise, when Peter Ellwood joined TSB as CEO Retail Banking in 1989 he wanted to understand accurately the context of the business, its strengths and its weaknesses. 'Ignore the past,' he warns, 'and you're in some peril.' What he discovered in 1989 was that many of the elements still remaining from TSB's old federal organization structure were a drag on performance. Up to 1976, for example, the bank still comprised 70 fairly autonomous savings banks. Despite public flotation in 1986, duplications across the retail banking business and fierce competition throughout the sector had resulted in 1989 operating costs growing at around 40 per cent per annum against revenue growth of 10 per cent.

To get to an accurate picture of the strengths and weaknesses of the business, Ellwood's leadership was tight, hands-on, absorbed in detail, 'crunching the numbers in every conceivable way,' as he puts it. He learned that TSB's strengths were:

- one of the largest customer bases in Europe (some 7 million customers);
- excellent branch banking information technology (IT);
- young and enthusiastic staff;
- a well-developed service culture; and
- strong empathy between staff and customers.

On the downside were:

- rising costs;
- duplication of functions and jobs;
- no long-term strategy; and
- a customer-base more elderly and down-market than competitors'.

All of this information taken together showed Ellwood what mattered, what the bank should be concentrating on. It meant TSB could be the people's bank. From this flowed the mission and strategy of TSB, with understanding and meeting customer needs as the priority and huge investments in people, branches, processes and systems to support the organizational transformation. On the evidence of the retail banking division's 1993 profits before tax of $726 million (in spite of recessionary conditions), London's *Daily Telegraph* was moved to comment: 'TSB's renaissance under newish chief executive Peter Ellwood has been little short of staggering'.

Disconnection

Being an outsider to a business can help in leading it. Since imposing context is so much about seeing the organization as it really is and how it should be, and then articulating for its members their place and role in achieving its objectives, the capacity to stand outside a business and view it warts and all is crucial. On the flip side of this are the great leaders whose terms at the top end in controversy and acrimony because they are blind to the problems of their own business; they have failed to stand apart, to disconnect.

Peter Ellwood was an outsider when he joined TSB. He saw the organization fresh, with the benefit of perspective. The danger for him, as he is all too aware, is to have feet of clay, to continue to concentrate his leadership on issues that mattered when radical transformation of the business was imperative, but are no longer relevant. With that behind him he is deliberately shifting both his leadership approach and the management structure that supports it. He sums it up this way:

> I have been schooling myself to take out my involvement in the levels of detail. Hitherto my approach was tight, hands-on: I knew everything I had to know. Now I'm trying to be more 'strategic' in the sense of being removed from the detail. Other people handle that ... It's not abdication. It's essential.

John Clark, arriving at BET in 1991 as its CEO, knew he was into a turnaround situation from the outset but, as he says, 'things are often going to be worse than they appear on the surface.' He found that the group's earning power was less than expected and it was vital to achieve financial stability. 'In many of my appointments,' he comments, 'the point of criticality has usually been reached when I come in: all the cash has been spent!' At BET restructuring, cost reduction and cash generation became the priorities.

However, John Clark saw BET moving into a new phase after the reorganization and cost reduction, something he calls 'total productivity'. Built on the right cost-base, this meant establishing the appropriate organizational culture and management system. It also meant a change in the types of issues he focused on. He explains:

> You need to adapt your leadership to the phases of the organizational lifecycle. When you're fixing the business, action-orientation, enthusiasm, leading from the front – all these are critical factors. And you have to get others to operate this way as well. Then in the new phase you must be more thoughtful, more strategic .... Above all, however, what matters is continually being able to look fresh at a business situation.

Robert van Gelder, Chairman of the Dutch group Royal Boskalis Westminster, says the same thing:

My colleagues and others worry about dredging techniques, projects, products, ships, equipment. That's their strength; they're very good at that. My background isn't dredging. I have to think about Boskalis as a business.

To that extent, van Gelder's background is a real plus. He can stand apart. He isn't constrained by the organization's bounds. He understands the business but he can think outside the box. This is crucial in a market that ten years ago could support 15 international players but now only six and where, as van Gelder reminds us, 'Boskalis nearly went belly-up in the mid-1980s because of over-diversification'.

Nevertheless, simply being part of the organization can gradually draw business leaders into a smothering embrace. In effect they become so thoroughly inducted that they lose all perspective. Dave Bowyer, Managing Director of Megapak, warns of this danger:

> At some point you begin to carry baggage – I mean getting too close to individuals or becoming involved in all the politics, not being objective. Before that happens you can still make dramatic changes on a much faster timescale than at any other time.

Making things happen by virtue of your disconnection with the business seems entirely at odds with the need to know the business in depth, but it isn't. Even (perhaps especially) in sluggish, bureaucratic institutions this disconnection is important. Hans Boom is the project manager for one of the largest rail construction initiatives in the European Community – the 160 kilometre Betuwe Line from Rotterdam to the German border. He has been given the job of planning and implementing the $4.4 billion project by the Dutch Ministry of Transport. Boom is, in his own words, 'an expert in managing large, complicated, politically complex projects,' and many years working within the Dutch civil service have equipped him with both a knowledge of the innards of government institutions and the political adroitness to work them effectively. But for several years now Boom has been an outsider, a consultant brought in to make things happen. He says:

> I'm an inside-outsider. I'm 'rented' for this job. Although I know a lot of people in government institutions, I'm not part of those institutions any more and I don't depend on the internal organization for my success. I've got nothing to lose or gain.

This is a great asset. The Dutch are a consensus people and so, of course, is their management – doubly so in the civil service. By extracting himself ('disconnecting') from the process of consensus management, he can be much bolder, more direct in the kinds of ways that create critical mass in the project. Most business leaders would kill to be able to see, understand and direct their organizations from such a position. The freedom, the release from internal political constraints, the opportunity to stand back and dissect the workings of a corporation with dispassion are huge advantages. None the less, such advantages are rarely granted to CEOs. They have to work within political constraints and shareholder pressures, but the lesson shouldn't be lost for all this. Leaders must still try to create the disconnection.

Churchill and Thatcher: political inside-outsiders

The great majority of the leaders of our political parties have been drawn from the mainstream of their respective traditions and cultures. As a result, you know roughly how, and where, they are going to lead their parties. Then, just occasionally, something interesting happens, usually as a result of desperation. A party elects a leader who comes from the edges of its tradition, who does not properly belong. Margaret Thatcher is the classic modern example, Winston Churchill an earlier instance. The relationship of such leaders with their parties is always uncomfortable, a little fraught. There is too much of the party they do not like, too many traditions, policies and habits they want to discard or transform.

Martin Jacques
'The adulation is over; the drama begins'
The Independent, 16 January 1995, p15

Clarity of Focus

Creating and imposing context, as we've already seen, is greatly dependent on the capacity of a leader to stand back and to have access to the right kinds of information. All of that is irrelevant, however, without the skill to synthesize and extract from a morass of market data, trends, political and social variables, and then fix on the core of what matters to the business. Precision is vital.

Senior colleagues soon sense uncertainty or confusion in their leaders and the sense of drift that takes hold among employees is frequently difficult to arrest.

Lotus Development Corporation started up in 1983, operating in a competitive and volatile software design market but Lotus CEO Jim Manzi was convinced that Lotus was a player in international markets and that the kinds of products that customers would want would be within an international context. Part of this involved developing and launching the new software product Lotus Notes, which would allow users to share information and customize the way information is seen and manipulated. People working in the same business, but in different locations, or in different worldwide businesses (for example vendors and clients) could therefore work better as a group, creating custom applications, sending and receiving messages or accessing multiple databases. This meant that Manzi had to ensure that Lotus employees were focused on the opportunity to meet global customers' needs.

There are now over one billion Lotus Notes users worldwide. Part of the reason for the success of Lotus Notes was the early and precise articulation of what the number one priority for Lotus was, and what failure would mean.

I have heard business leaders call this simply 'clarity of focus'. What they mean is that their job, as president and CEO, or as a business unit head or as the leader of any organizational grouping, is to make certain that all employees understand where they're going, or, indeed, where they're not going. In imposing context, stating clearly what your business is not concerned with can be just as important as precision of objectives. 'In most transformation cases I've been involved in,' John Clark says, 'you must decide the businesses that you want to be in *and* gain focus through the *exclusion* of markets and businesses which are not a good fit. That may mean selling business units because of the market conditions or because of the management talent available.'

In many industries the pressure to go global is becoming intense. However, John McCoy, Chairman at Banc One Corporation in the US, sounds a note of caution:

> There is no reason for us to go global … . We've made a lot of money just getting into 13 states … . We'll be far better off to try to get into the other 37 before we go to London and Madrid … . Our *customers* are not globally oriented.

To go global or not to go global? Knowing the answer to this is easy enough. Usually your customers will be pointing the way and the best business leaders intimately know their customers. Articulating this context is more difficult though, not least because it involves persuading others.

Articulating Nationhood

In 1985, still imprisoned, Nelson Mandela made a fateful decision: to begin discussions with the South African government. 'I chose to tell no one what I was about to do,' he writes in his autobiography *Long Walk to Freedom* (1994). 'Not my colleagues upstairs nor those in Lusaka ... . I knew that my colleagues upstairs would condemn my proposal, and that would kill my initiative even before it was born. There are times when a leader must move out ahead of the flock, go off in a new direction, confident that he is leading his people the right way.' (p 514)

On 10 May 1994 Mandela was sworn in as President of South Africa and addressed the nation:

'Today, all of us do, by our presence here, and by our celebrations in other parts of our country and the world, confer glory and hope to newborn liberty. Out of the experience of an extraordinary human disaster that lasted too long, must be born a society of which all humanity will be proud ... .

'The time for the healing of the wounds has come. The moment to bridge the chasms that divide us has come. The time to build is upon us ... .

'We have triumphed in the effort to implant hope in the breasts of the millions of our people. We enter into a covenant that we shall build the society in which all South Africans, both black and white, will be able to walk tall, without any fear in their hearts, assured of their inalienable right to human dignity – a rainbow nation at peace with itself and the world ... .

'Never, never and never again shall it be that this beautiful land will again experience the oppression of one by another and suffer the indignity of being the skunk of the world.

'Let freedom reign. The sun shall never set on so glorious a human achievement.'

Extracts from the speech of Nelson Mandela, sworn in on 10 May 1994 as President of South Africa.

The New Context

Try to run an organization within a business, political and social environment in the throes of change on a scale equivalent to that of the earth's tectonic plates grinding together and you might be forgiven for simply packing up and going home and forgetting about this thing called leadership. In South Africa, and perhaps nowhere else quite like it in the world, business leaders are confronted by seemingly insurmountable challenges. I talked to three business leaders, two Black and one White, in the months following the historic multi-party elections in that country, knowing that in the new South Africa leadership bears a very heavy burden, but that here of all places the complex lessons of leadership could be profound.

Koos Radebe is one of a small number of emerging Black business leaders. As General Manager for Commercial Radio at the South African Broadcasting Corporation his role is at the focal point of a society still largely divided, economically and socially. He is also in the front-line of sweeping affirmative action, but is tasked with delivering commercially viable radio services to a polyglot community. Nonetheless, he is clear about the context. 'We are here, in a sense,' he states, 'to bring people together.'

Sounds like a slogan? Yes. But bringing people together is the problem South Africa faces – both in its broadest scope and between one individual and another. On their own, of course, slogans carry little force. In his business Radebe has imposed context by being precise about what it means to bring people together, how that will happen in the organization, where each employee stands. He gives this account:

> When I was appointed, I called a meeting of all staff and talked to them to set the vision for what we need to achieve. Three things: co-operation, acceptance of diversity of cultures, but in the workplace one common purpose: survival … . We have to make the job far bigger than ourselves, otherwise we won't *have* any jobs.

Junior Potloane, a General Manager within Nedcor Bank, is faced by similar challenges, in his case how to create a 'People's Bank' in a country where a large proportion of the Black population do not use banks. In Potloane's view his job is to 'make banking accessible to the unbanked majority.' This is extraordinarily difficult. Banks are slow, cautious and averse to risk-taking. Received wisdom in South Africa holds that bringing banking services to the 'unbanked majority' is high risk and low-return. Moreover, there are few who understand what the Black banking market looks like, still less how to draw into the wider banking network the millions of Black consumers who rely exclusively on cash as their payment mechanism. To make any progress at all, Potloane has had to be absolutely clear about the context:

> There is a lot of resistance, not to say fear, in the Group to the idea. I'm trying to turn this round: I have to focus people heavily on the opportunities in this emerging market, as well as the risks of not getting into it. We either move forward or the government will *impose* regulations that force us to play a role in that market, or the business will go to other financial services players.

Potloane is doing two things: disconnecting, so that colleagues can see the business from another perspective, from the outside; and bringing focus to the bank's new role. Although he recognizes that a strategic plan for achieving this is important, he says that it is much less important than communicating 'a composite or holistic view of the end product, no matter how far ahead'. In other words, he is in the business of creating a sea-change within the bank, inspiring some, persuading others to recognize and to adopt the idea of banking for the unbanked majority.

At another level, as South Africa has broken out of the isolation that has retarded its growth and opportunities, businesses have come hard up against a highly competitive international business arena, something from which they were largely insulated during preceding decades. Megapak's Dave Bowyer gives an insight into this:

> Many South African businesses don't have a global perspective. And we know we cannot exist with a parochial market view. We're trying to accomplish a huge mind-set change from protectionism with no, or very little, competition when customers were simply not getting what they wanted, to competing against the biggest and best players in the world … . We need to get beyond just a Southern African perspective to an international perspective – and in Megapak we're eyeing the huge market in China, for example.

New into the job, Bowyer had to make it plain to his management team and workers exactly where they stood in this abruptly different world. Unfortunately, history wasn't on his side. His predecessor's autocratic style had restricted the flow of information and power to a small group of managers at the top. Even after Bowyer took over the reins, the long-established culture allowed other managers in the business the ready excuse that they weren't ever fully in the picture and therefore couldn't be expected to make things happen. Bowyer needed a trigger for change. He describes how he tackled it:

> One of our businesses had been loss-making for years. I announced that we had one year to turn it round. Otherwise, on such-and-such a date, a year from now, we close it down.

The message was clear. Here was the new context.

A similar dramatic shift in culture has been driven by many CEOs of firms in hi-tech and engineering industries. Varian Associates in the US and British Aerospace in the UK are cases in point. Varian, one of the first hi-tech companies set up some 45 years ago in what became Silicon Valley, had an outstanding capability in technology development but by the late 1980s none of the myriad business units really possessed sufficient critical mass to operate efficiently and profitably. Moreover, the culture of Varian was predominantly 'scientific' rather than business driven. Varian was slowly losing market share. Its new Chairman, Tracy O'Rourke, had to make it clear what the new context was – although the business was concerned with 'scientific' development, it also had to be business driven, and everyone had to understand that and operate in a way very different from before.

Similarly, British Aerospace, like many firms with a history of sophisticated engineering design and development, has had to shift the emphasis from attaining excellence in engineering at all costs to excellence in engineering at the right cost and at the right time. The change is pushed hard from the top. It must be plain that the leaders of a firm wholeheartedly believe in it.

In ensuring that this kind of shift to the acceptance of a new context takes hold, business leaders must be aware of the tradition and history that they're up against. They must also be able to articulate compelling reasons for the shift. Ford's Alex Trotman, for example, insists:

> Companies that aren't globally competitive are going to be out of business or swallowed up by other companies.

What these stories illustrate is that leadership is day-to-day. You cannot set the company going then stand back and watch it. Imposing context is as much about constant personal communication and example as about recognizing and articulating focus to one's team and to the entire organization. As we have already seen, slogans, watchwords and mission statements inspire no one unless leaders bring them to life in word and action.

Sound-bite Leadership

In the two years leading up to the 1994 US mid-term elections, President Clinton attempted to shift his appeal onto a broader base. Traditional Democrats have typically been unionized workers, African Americans, single women and elderly voters. Clinton wanted to capture those who voted for Ross Perot in the 1992 election, generally white middle-class males. He also became something of a sound-bite President, so conscious of the power of the media and the pollsters that policy measures seemed to be constructed and adjusted as rapidly and carelessly as the media's appetite for novelty.

Clinton was rewarded with a mid-term catastrophe, one of the worst mid-term reverses in US political history. What went wrong?

Clinton failed to impose context. Voters were left confused: what did the Democrats stand for? This week? Next week? Next year? What did Clinton stand for? What should the voters themselves stand for? Clinton had moved the Democrats so quickly to the political centre, trying to reconcile the apparently irreconcilable, that he lost the traditional vote without converting any new constituencies.

People, in any country, of whatever ideological hue, will not tolerate for long the vague and the fuzzy, the uncertain and the inconsistent. They want meaning imposed. They want to understand the context. They want leadership.

SUMMARY

Imposing Context

1 *Information*: access it (past, present, future); crunch the numbers in every conceivable way.

2 *Disconnection*: stand apart, be an inside-outsider and understand your business as it is and as it should be.

3 *Clarity of focus*: be precise. Know where you're going and where you're not going.

4 *Cut through the noise*: make it clear what matters and what does not, in spite of conflicting messages from elsewhere. Bring the context to life through your own action.

4

RISK MAKING, RISK TAKING

Fighting Fires

In February 1995, Nick Leeson, a derivatives trader in the Singa-pore office of Britain's oldest merchant banking group Barings, bought Nikkei futures contracts in a gamble on a rebound of the Tokyo stock market. Leeson, by all accounts, was acting well beyond his formal authority. The market fell further. Barings, exposed to losses of around $1.5 billion, could not be bailed out and the administrators were called in. An institution founded in 1762 faced ruin.

No one would argue that the global business environment is a risky place. More diverse, uncharted and geographically spread markets, increasing competitive pressure and financial volatility are all factors confronting business leaders. Concomitantly, busi-ness failures, setbacks and frauds, of the kind illustrated in the Barings fiasco, have tended to prompt internal organizational systems for managing risk, with the result that risk management processes, corporate governance and pre-emptive internal control have become standards in many large organizations. Let's be honest: most organizations need lots of control, be it centralized and process-driven or empowered and person-dependent. Big or small, organizations make mistakes, lack data, are taken by sur-prise, or simply get tired. Control provides the comfort for leaders to concentrate on things other than fighting fires. But control can go way too far, particularly where it affects leadership roles. The danger is everpresent.

We can see this at a national level in Germany. Hard on the heels of the shock of early 1990s recession and accompanying restructuring, many German organizations, particularly in hi-tech industries such as IT and biotechnology, have become anxious about Germany falling far behind in the twenty-first century's new technology race. Fewer research ideas are making the transformation to saleable products, patent registrations have declined and the strains of German reunification have until recently tightened fiscal purse strings for technological research. Beneath all this it is not hard to uncover in German industry the intense dedication to control, rules, planning and reliability that has been a substantial part of the country's post-war success, but which, in its obverse (inflexibility, scepticism, unwillingness to take risks), may mean its industrial decline in a new global economic pecking order. (See the section *High achieving risk-takers* towards the end of this chapter for some comparative evidence on the German proclivity to avoid risks.)

Control equals right first time. That meant success in the 1980s and early 1990s. It will mean partial success in the new millennium. Why? Because in the past quality/right first time was a significant differentiator that gradually sorted out the success stories from the also-rans. Now, quality/right first time is seen by the market as a given. It is expected. Therefore, being as good as you've been for the last year – controlling things – is no longer good enough. Better, cheaper, faster processes; new products, more fashionable products; other markets; other countries; being different, adding value to the business – these are the things that will count. It is the job of leaders (in the example above, German politicians and industrialists) to identify opportunities and take risks, or at the very least to encourage it in others. The problem with risks is twofold: you can't really plan to take risks (there are few rules) and scepticism doesn't help. Yes, organizations should do it right first time, but leaders shouldn't. Leaders must try things, make mistakes, take risks.

Risk Making, Risk Taking

Peter Drucker, one of the world's foremost management gurus, states that any economic activity commits resources in the present to the uncertainty of the future. In his book *Management* (1977) he also refers to a principle of economics (Boehm-Bawerk's Law) which proves that 'existing means of production will yield greater economic performance only through greater uncertainty, that is, through greater risk.' (p 119)

It requires no leap of faith therefore to grasp the fact that you cannot run an enterprise without risk. This applies just as well to leaders of business units, projects, departments, as it does to CEOs. In a volatile business world, playing it safe, sticking to the tried and tested, controlling things, is a guarantee of mediocrity, no matter what part of the organization you lead. A leader's thoughts therefore must be focused on opportunity. Opportunity, as Figure 4.1 shows, springs from the questions of context: Where are we going? Where are we not going? From those questions arises the periodic, hard-nosed analysis of the organization that all leaders must perform:

- What things must I change?
  - processes;
  - projects;
  - markets; and
  - activities.
- How do I change it/shut it down/pull the plug/divest?
- What new things can I try and when?

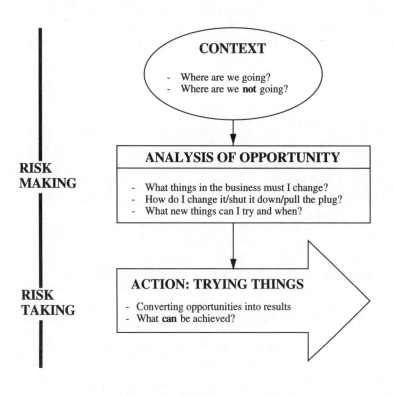

Figure 4.1 *Risk making, risk taking*

However, analysis of opportunity is only half the story. It is risk making. Risk taking, by contrast, goes much further and is aimed at *converting* opportunities into results. It is where the rules and the plans with which we might try to attack opportunity break down, where leadership becomes all important. It is where control and scepticism become very dangerous, where conviction and the belief in what *can* be achieved are paramount and the simple expedient of *trying things* is vital.

Opportunity

Leadership gets ordinary people to do extraordinary things. Life in general for the vast majority of people is ordinary. EM Forster, author of *A Passage to India* (1924), wrote:

> Most of life is so dull that there is nothing to be said about it, and the books and talk that would describe it as interesting are obliged to exaggerate, in the hope of justifying their own existence. Inside its cocoon of work or social obligation, the human spirit slumbers for the most part, registering the distinction between pleasure and pain, but not nearly as alert as we pretend. There are periods in the most thrilling day during which nothing happens, and though we continue to exclaim, 'I do enjoy myself', or, 'I am horrified', we are insincere. (p 132)

How many of us can honestly dispute this? It is for this very reason that leaders are important. Leaders show us the opportunities, at the very least, for performing better than we believe we are capable. But each time they do, they confront us with risk. Change is personally risky, even though the rewards can be great. Alex Trotman at Ford says:

> The best work we've done probably is the work we didn't think we could do ... . One of the best examples we've had in recent years is our five-point market share gain in the United States market of total car and truck sales ... . I don't think you'd find anyone in Ford today who could honestly tell you that back in 1980 we could have got five points of market share.

Opportunities are the risks it would be easier (and 'safer') to avoid, but let's not be tempted to imagine that opportunities are simply 'things out there' which once in a while you will chance upon or winkle out. Leaders create risks through the analysis of opportunity. Indeed, without the individual even seeking it, the job of

being a leader creates what we might call psychological space –
the freedom to act – which in turn brings risk. As Peter Ellwood
of TSB says, 'Senior roles are largely about risk. We must understand risk, not remove it. If we remove risk, we remove profit.'
The same view is echoed by Robert van Gelder at Boskalis, but
with the emphasis firmly on the active creation of opportunity
and risk:

> Opportunities should serve the future of this company. I am
> always the one who is forcing the organization to think non-tra-
> ditionally. For example, everyone believes that technology pro-
> vides a competitive advantage. But in dredging our technology
> isn't different from 20 years ago. It doesn't offer an advantage to
> refurbish or renew. I want people to think about mergers, alliances
> – different ideas.

For those who are unused to it or inadequate to senior roles, such
freedom can spell disaster. Alex Watson, President and CEO of
Chep in Europe, acknowledges the value of psychological space
but gives a warning:

> I've been used to space all my life. But space brings risk. I've seen
> it in my own managers ... and you need to stay sufficiently close
> that you sense the size of risk they are faced with and can help out,
> without breathing down people's necks.

Pushing this thinking down the organization (or harder still, into
subsidiaries) makes for considerable success – if you can do it.
Banc One *must* do this. As an acquisitive corporation with more
than 80 separate banks under its aegis, you can't exercise total
control, you can't force managers to introduce identical processes
in what were different institutions. But you can encourage people
to take the responsibility to recognize or seek out opportunities
for improvement and make the changes themselves. John McCoy
explains:

> If I *told* you to take out 100 people, you might just want to prove
> me wrong, so you'd fire the best 100 people so that at the end of
> the year you could say: 'It didn't work, McCoy!' ... . If I tell
> everybody what to do or their boss tells them what to do, then
> there's a lack of innovation in the company: nobody's willing to
> try anything.

Pulling the Plug – but not Eating the Young

Take a hard look at your own organization. How many projects, initiatives, processes, or activities are there that should have been shut down a long time ago? (If you think there is none, you're fooling yourself.) The measure of whether they should have been shut down is, quite simply, whether they are still productive.

Too many corporations, however, are obese. Obsolete processes and systems, more often than not, persist because they provide a justification for someone's daily activity or because 'it's always been that way'! How many new IT applications, developed and implemented at one time in the distant past to serve the specific needs of end-users at the sharp end of the business, just grow and grow in staff and cost, amoeba-like, until they take on a life of their own? How many projects attract specialists and consultants dedicated only to serving the further survival of the project, even though the end-users have long since been making alternative arrangements?

Far too infrequently do senior managers have the courage to suspend initiatives, to pull the plug on ponderous development projects that are not delivering, or even take action when the wrong person has been backed for a crucial role. Nelson Robertson at General Accident describes the problem:

> We have sometimes persevered too long with people who have not really got the capacity to rise. We have failed to stop things early enough – when there were warning signs.

The action of acknowledging an error, no matter how large, produces new ways of looking at things: 'Yes, we've got it wrong. Now, what do we do next? How do we do it?'. The trouble is many senior managers never build the support framework to enable them to take that first step of acknowledging the failure. They are too embarrassed. They will lose face. They will be seen as weak. They will lose respect. Moreover, the longer you leave it, the harder it gets. Alex Trotman sums up the approach in the senior team at Ford, an approach so essential for the success of the large changes the company is making:

> We're not writing a prescription in stone … . One of the commitments we made to each other as a management team was that, as we move forward and as we find that we've made mistakes in organization concepts, process concepts or in terms of appointing people to jobs, we have to acknowledge the mistakes very quickly and make the change very quickly – adjust as we go along.

Trotman is describing, if you like, a culture change in the top team. To make it easier and more effective to acknowledge mistakes, leaders need to produce a shift between:

Old top team culture	*New top team culture*
I always get decisions right.	We all make mistakes.
My job is to avoid mistakes.	My job is to take risks.
Shoot the messenger. Don't talk failure.	If it's failing, why?
If it's wrong, maybe it'll get better.	If it's wrong, change it.

The objection: easy to talk about, hard to do. Certainly, but like any other business process it must have rules and a structure (as straightforward, even, as the above). It must be agreed in the top team and then implemented. After all, it's only a new way of doing things. None the less, I've heard senior teams complain bitterly that it'll never succeed, usually with the same old lame excuse that 'it's not the way it works round here'. But the very same senior team will quite happily demand equivalent behaviour change of their subordinates. Who says the executive team is immune? The executives, unfortunately.

It is the job of leaders to make change happen around them, particularly in their own team, and not allow themselves to be cut off from accurate information on results or isolated from the honest feedback of their team. As we shall later see, this is, perhaps, the greatest danger of all for a leader.

Pulling the plug, of course, should be balanced against the need to preserve fledgling products, projects and ideas from the proclivity of the organization to 'eat its young'. People resist new notions. They protect *their* product line or *their* business unit with the same solidarity and ferocity as warring tribes (see *In-group, out-group* box below). The underlying driving force for this behaviour (in businesses as in tribes) is competition for scarce resources. Business units in big organizations are *always* competing for resources. Leaders therefore assume a difficult dual role of executioner (pulling the plug) and guardian angel, where new ideas need to be protected from premature and destructive criticism or action.

In-group, Out-group

A series of studies, famous in social psychology, illustrates the powerful effects of inter-group hostility, conflict and co-operation. The tendency for people to think and act in 'us' and 'them' terms is more fundamental than we might imagine, and is typically associated with the belief that 'we' are (for no rational reason) better than 'them'.

Muzafer Sherif and a number of colleagues demonstrated in their experiments that the mere fact of introducing competition between different groups of people very quickly produces not just rivalry but open hostility and aggression. They also found, surprisingly, that, even after the need for competition has been removed, individuals from the separate groups will have nothing to do with each other. At the same time, in-group solidarity (loyalty to the group) becomes cherished.

The good news is that Sherif also showed how inter-group conflict could be reduced, although the process is almost always difficult. What works least well (which is not at all) are the informational campaigns designed to persuade different groups to co-operate, or appeals to individuals to change. People pay lip-service, then at once return to hostility to other groups. What works best is introducing shared, superordinate goals or initiating co-operative projects. Which happens to be one of the tasks of leadership.

See Sherif and Sherif (1953); Sherif *et al* (1955); Sherif *et al* (1961) and Tajfel (1970, 1981)

Kick the Beast

The Post Office in Great Britain has its origins in the Royal postal services operated by fifteenth century kings. Opened to the public in 1635, the modern Post Office can look back on 360 years of business and, as Chief Executive Bill Cockburn reminds us, 'all of that history and tradition ... part of the social fabric of the country'. But all of that tradition can act as an enormous counterweight to business-driven change. Cockburn is unequivocal about both context and risk:

> We aspire to world-class status: we have explored and benchmarked business processes in Xerox, Motorola, IBM and so forth.

We ourselves are a benchmark organization worldwide for post office businesses and we are the most profitable post office in the world ... . [However,] there is deep risk-aversion in the Post Office.

To that extent, Cockburn has had to be even bolder in his own risk-taking and has insisted that the organization embrace more change in the last five years than it has experienced in the last 50. He goes on:

Sometimes ... there has been no immediate need for change or the changes are looked upon as reckless, particularly where we've reorganized and cut overheads ... but I think it's a bit like pruning roses: it provides a surge in growth ... . Making those changes has given me a lot of confidence. I've learned you can really kick the beast and not damage it. The fact is, not enough businesses are bold enough ... . In spite of advice to the contrary, I never believed [the change initiatives] would fail.

Like Banc One it has been a priority in the Post Office to push the responsibility for initiating and leading change down through the business. Couched within a framework of total quality, this manifests itself in the Post Office's Leadership Commitment, a statement of the expected standards for leadership actions and behaviour for anyone in the business in a leadership role, whether in fixed teams or projects. There are ten key actions to which leaders commit, supported by regular feedback (both self-assessed and by team members).

The Post Office: Leadership Commitment

Team leaders visibly:

1 Set a clear focus on external and internal customers' requirements.

2 Set goals which support the mission and vision.

3 Understand and demonstrate commitment to business policies.

4 Set a strong personal example of enthusiasm, drive and co-operation.

5 Regularly measure, communicate and recognize team performance.

6 Make objective decisions based on facts.

---

7   Seek solutions, not problems, and encourage positive and imaginative thinking.

8   Encourage people to work in teams and to co-operate with other teams.

9   Develop and recognize team members as individuals.

10   Communicate openly and honestly and listen to feedback.

Action 7 spells out a credo that every organization in the 1990s should try to live by. Given in full, in behavioural terms, it's about:

- Looking actively to solve problems rather than being defeated by them.
- Encouraging flexibility in meeting changing customer requirements.
- Being prepared to break with convention when required.
- Delegating decision-making regularly, within clear boundaries, and encouraging the use of initiative.
- Treating failure positively, and emphasizing the learning points in all situations.
- Encouraging positive thinking.
- Listening to ideas.

Yes, I know it's a wish-list. But Bill Cockburn is *serious* about those actions. His senior managers are serious about them too. One of Cockburn's team, Bob Peaple, Director of Resources of Post Office Counters, sums it up this way: 'If you're not making mistakes, you're not *doing* anything.'

So, you ask, I have to go out and make mistakes? Well, yes. Hence, the risk. Leaders are in earnest about this. Bill Cockburn again: 'I'm forever encouraging managers to look outwards to see what the competition is doing, to benchmark against the best and then try things. Our catering unit used to be an overhead and inefficient. Now they're winning external contracts.' John Clark of BET says it best:

It's what I call creative plagiarism – being constantly well read. I spend a total of at least half-a-day a week reading as much as I can – periodicals, briefings, books. At some point in time I get a paragraph that turns on a light that eventually solves a problem in business X or Y.

That preparedness to try new or different things (often things that fly in the face of conventional wisdom or, indeed, fashion) is sometimes a large part of the individual's make-up. Ian Preston of Scottish Power, as a case in point, says, 'I wanted to get away from working *for* others, get away from the constraints that that imposes, have the autonomy to *do* things differently.' But it's not immutable; it's not simply a personality characteristic that you either have or you don't. Leaders can develop it incrementally. Alex Watson of Chep in Europe said to me:

> Learning how to win in small things during your life and career teaches you leadership. But leaders have to be winners of big events. They have to make a difference at a critical time. So you have to practise winning and your people do too. This brings self-belief and confidence.

The action of trying things, of converting opportunities into results, hinges on a moment of decision, an instant that can have enormous consequences, not just immediately by virtue of the action it produces now, but through its medium and long-term implications. Equally, refusing to take a decision, remember, is a decision of a kind, though often with unpredictable (not to say irrevocable) consequences. When it comes to risk, leaders are able to make decisions, usually fast, and on many occasions almost revelling in it. Dave Bowyer of Megapak:

> I've always been able to make decisions fast, and sometimes I've made decisions way *beyond* my authority – to the extent that the decision would either have got me promoted or fired! But quite frankly, people respect you if you have the balls to make a tough decision.

Sense any fear of failure in that statement? Absolutely. Every business leader I've spoken to fears failure, but they don't allow it to interfere with the willingness to experiment and take risks, at the personal and organizational level. In *The Change Masters* (1983), Rosabeth Moss Kanter makes the point in a different way:

> What an innovating organization does is open up action possibilities rather than restrict them and thus trusts to faith as well as formal plans. A well-managed innovating organization clearly has plans – mission, strategies, structure, central thrust, a preference for some activities/products/markets over others – but it also has a willingness to reconceptualize the details and even sometimes the overarching frameworks on the basis of continual accumulation of new ideas – innovations – produced by its people, both as individuals and as members of participating teams. (p 306)

But from where does this willingness to reconceptualize come? New ideas, innovations – risk-taking – start with leadership, with taking tough decisions and going beyond the limits of authority or formal plans. Leaders who play it safe and who expect their organizations to play it safe may get by, but their organizations won't.

What is surprising, in a business world that typically trusts to formality, systems and plans – 'the numbers' – is the extent to which successful business leaders trust the opposite – faith. One executive, describing the initiation of an organization-wide change programme, told me once: 'A "strategic" decision to change is usually nothing more than gut-feel dressed up in numbers and rubber-stamped by some committee.' Was he oversimplifying? No. The process of rubber-stamping may absorb committee time and involve mountains of paperwork and begin to look like the strategic decision itself, but it rarely is.

Hamel and Prahalad, in their 1994 ground-breaking book *Competing for the Future*, lambast the devaluation of strategy in modern organizations, asserting that it has come to mean 'incremental tactical planning punctuated by heroic, and usually ill-conceived, "strategic" investments'. (p 281) Their concern is that strategy fails to prompt the deeper debates of what and how and why about a firm's future. It doesn't deal with 'white space opportunities' and is hopelessly incrementalist.

They argue that:

> To extend industry foresight and develop a supporting strategic architecture, companies need a new perspective on what it means to be 'strategic'. They need to ask new strategy questions: not just how to maximize share and profits in today's businesses, but who do we want to be as a corporation in ten years' time, how can we reshape this industry to our advantage, what new functionalities do we want to create for customers, and what new core competencies should we be building? They need a new process for strategy-making, one that is more exploratory and less ritualistic. They need to apply new and different resources to the task of strategy-making, relying on the creativity of hundreds of managers and not just on the wisdom of a few planners. (p 282)

This is not meant to denigrate the value of rigorous analysis, the careful consideration of options, risk identification and monitoring. All of these things have their place. But no amount of analysis – on its own – will produce the right strategic decision. It may even produce the wrong one, for two reasons: first, we simply cannot know everything; second, the future (unless you are a determinist or have read too many Greek tragedies) can be made to happen.

In the first instance, that requires information and judgement; in the second instance, plain hard work.

High-Achieving Risk Takers

Do CEOs regularly bet the company? Do high achievers take high risks?

No. It is a misconception that great leaders take great risks, although in different cultures managers have different tolerances for risk taking. David McClelland, a Harvard psychologist, showed that low and high achievers behave quite differently when taking risks (1961). Low achievers do one of two things: either they minimize risk as much as possible or they take wild, irrational risks. High achievers, by contrast, typically take moderate risks, but the nub of it is that they calculate risks against circumstances and their own abilities. As crazy as some business leaders' risk-taking may often seem, closer inspection will usually show you careful (albeit highly intuitive) calculation of risks that are not so crazy after all.

Different cultures, however, have more or less tolerance for risk taking, and produce managers accordingly. American managers have a very high tolerance for risk whereas the Germans and Belgians have a much lower tolerance.

Managers' risk tolerance in different countries

	Percent
United States	89
Japan	67
Netherlands	61
France	61
Scandinavia	61
Latin America	60
Britain	50
India	50
Italy	44
Iberia	44
Belgium	39
Germany–Austria	39

From Bass and Burger (1979, p91)

SUMMARY

Risk Making, Risk Taking

1 *Risk making*: what things must I change? How do I change it/shut it down/pull the plug/divest? What new things can I try and when?

2 *Opportunity*: understand risk, don't remove it.

3 *Pull the plug*: if it's failing, why? If it's wrong, change it. But don't let the organization eat its young.

4 *Kick the beast*: if you're not making mistakes, you're not *doing* anything. Take the risk. The organization is tougher than you think. So are you.

5

UNPREDICTABILITY

Corporate Inventiveness: Moving Outside the Pattern

The organizations we work in, the careers we follow, the work we do, all – almost without exception – foster homogeneity, logic, structure, predictability. It is hardly to our discredit as humans that we prefer a mechanistic, predictable vision of society and business. Machines and mechanical modes of thought have brought us enormous benefits. When the industrial revolution began in Britain in the 1700s, the face of society and work changed forever. Lawrence James reports in *The Rise and Fall of the British Empire* (1994) that in 1801 there were about 10 million people in Britain. Seventy years later there were 22 million. Without the industrial revolution millions would have starved. Moreover, by 1880 the country's industrial lead had secured it nearly a quarter of world trade and a third of world output.

But the intellectual force behind the industrial revolution was not just about logic, structure and predictability. Entrepreneurial spirit, inventiveness, risk – the unpredictable – were the true hallmarks of technological and industrial advance. Even before the turn of the century Britain had begun to lag behind the United States and Germany in developing new technologies and production methods. Britain's inventiveness had stagnated. It may be in the nature of societies that this happens; perhaps, when nations become economically successful and then dominant, the burden of maintaining dominance distracts from innovation, new technological development and further economic progress. There are numerous examples in history – Egypt, the Greeks, Rome. It seems certain that the United States is likewise experiencing long-term decline. From pre-eminence in 1950 (contributing nearly half of world output) America has slipped to below 25 per cent. This corporate stagnation has directly prompted the series of best-selling management books from the US since the 1970s. In 1983 in *The Change Masters* Rosabeth Moss Kanter even posed the question: Can America do it? Can America realize a corporate renaissance?

The question is moot, or irrelevant. It could be that the growing global market has made questions about any country's corporate renaissance much less important than the capacity of managements to structure and operate truly global businesses, regardless of nationality. In other words, what is important is how successful organizations are at winning in an interdependent global economy through dynamic networks linking countries, institutions and people, particularly within the TRIAD trading blocs (Western Europe, Asia and North America). 'Today, if you look closely at the world TRIAD companies inhabit,' wrote Kenichi Ohmae in *The Borderless World* (1990), 'national borders have effectively disappeared and, along with them, the economic logic that made them useful lines of demarcation in the first place.'

The world, as I said in Chapter 1, is different. What isn't different, though, is the intellectual force that first drove the industrial revolution in Britain, that fired American entrepreneurs and that has stimulated the huge growth of Japan and now the Asian Dragons: inventiveness, seizing upon opportunity and turning it to commercial advantage. In the previous chapter we saw one aspect of the role of leaders in this respect – their capacity to create and take risks. There is another; the willingness to go beyond the norm, challenge the status quo, to move outside the pattern – unpredictability. For some leaders this is manifest in unpredictability in personal style; for others, in their adeptness at changing strategic tack or jolting the organization out of a rut. I have called it 'unpredictability' because it is a quality that grabs attention and that turns heads in organizations that are mostly logical, rational, formal, uniform, sometimes unchanging, even (dare we admit it?) boring. When leaders are a saviour of a declining business when a saviour is called for, expand when expansion is required, revitalize when revitalization is needed, we make such attributions after the fact, as if they were an explanation, when what we are really grasping after as the chief cause is the quality of unpredictability in a particular leader, doing things that few others might have predicted. You might call this creativity and creativity may be part of it, but there are numerous leaders who are neither creative nor particularly imaginative; it is just that they have the capacity to do the unpredictable.

Show More Goodly and Attract More Eyes

If all the year were playing holidays,
To sport would be as tedious as to work;
But when they seldom come, they wish'd for come,
And nothing pleaseth but rare accidents.
So, when this loose behaviour I throw off,
And pay the debt I never promised,
By how much better than my word I am,
By so much shall I falsify men's hopes;
And, like bright metal on a sullen ground,
My reformation, glittering o'er my fault,
Shall show more goodly, and attract more eyes,
Than that which hath no foil to set it off.
I'll so offend, to make offence a skill;
Redeeming time, when men think least I will.

William Shakespeare
(Prince Henry in *The First Part of King Henry IV*)

Adventure!

'If there aren't any threats or impending disasters,' says Hans Boom, 'then I create them. As a matter of course I try to create adventure.' (Interestingly, Bill Cockburn uses the same word – adventure – about institutionalizing change.) One of the reasons Boom creates adventure is because he enjoys it. He hates routine and delights in change. By his own admission he takes his motorcycle from the Netherlands to Germany and drives as fast as he can on the autobahns. The other reason for creating adventure (or imminent disaster, depending on your perspective) is that it produces action. It is a trigger for change.

Homo sapiens occupies a bewilderingly diverse range of environments across the globe. Over the past millenia we have been marvellously successful at adapting to the pressures of our environment. People do much the same in organizations, by and large responding to what the corporate environment (its culture rather than the formal entity) expects of them, with remarkably few extremes of behaviour, that is, doing neither too little nor too much. Slow, bureaucratic, hierarchical businesses produce – surprise, surprise – slow, bureaucratic behaviour. The oddballs who don't fit, move out – but they are rare. It is no great shock, therefore, that people need a reason, a justification, to change, that they need to be pushed. Impending disaster – real or deliberately created – provides a justification and a push. It is true that people respond more favourably to change when there is a compelling reason to do so. Hans Boom, for instance, used the threat of privatization in government institutions in the Netherlands to improve performance radically. Privatization itself, popular across Western and now Eastern Europe and indeed all over the world, can initiate profound changes in colossal state-owned agencies; witness the success of British Airways over the 1980s, or more recently Lufthansa, moving from daily million dollar losses and the brink of disaster three years ago to a successful rights issue in September 1994, prior to the completion of privatization in 1995.

From the perspective of leadership, however, it is the *imminence* of change that is of interest. Inducing crisis, or the threat of it, brings sufficient uncertainty among employees to enable leaders to make change happen. It used to be that new management ideas such as organization development (OD) and total quality management (TQM) were sufficient to provide a fresh trigger for change at an appropriate time, but they have been both overdone by over-eager managements impressed by their technical wizardry and poorly implemented, frequently without the stewardship of senior executives. *The Economist* (14 January 1995) reports on the increasing tussle in corporate America between TQM and the pressure to downsize, restructure and re-engineer. At heart the former emphasizes ongoing, step-by-step improvements, whereas the latter is a commitment to wholesale, quantum change in business processes. An additional wrinkle on the problem is the never-ending demand for reducing new product time-to-market. Apart from the internal organizational strains this sets off, it also interferes with many quality processes. In the 1990s, when jaundiced employees have experienced half-a-dozen or more of what in their eyes may be seen as 'change fads' (most with only varying degrees of success), patience wears thin. The truth is, new management initiatives don't work without leadership and fads are no substitute for leadership.

Leadership should make change initiatives less of a burden and more of an adventure. Several of the business leaders I interviewed mentioned the value of experiments and pilots, particularly where employees were given the responsibility to try things out and learn from them. That is unpredictability embraced, active encouragement to employees to take risks and to deal with the market and the organizational world in unpredictable ways in order to learn what works best.

John McCoy at Banc One relates this anecdote:

> I'd like to tell you that the reason we're the third largest credit card processor in the United States is that we drew a strategic plan. We didn't draw a strategic plan. A bank in Newark, Ohio, thirty miles down the road, came up and said: 'You're in the credit card business. Could you help us to get to the business?' We thought maybe we'd like to buy them, so we put them into the business. No strategic plan. We just stumbled on it.

That too is about embracing unpredictability. Yet almost in the same breath McCoy can warn, 'Everybody wants to go off and do the new thing, whereas I'm much more: "Let's go back and do what we're doing even better".' Paradox it may be, but it is not fuzzy thinking. It is the job of leaders to build stable organizations that are flexible, that can deal with the unpredictable. Striking the balance is a matter of judgement. Derek Wanless at NatWest talks about the leader's role in 'absorbing uncertainty' where uncertainty is destructive, damaging motivation. More on this in Chapter 6 where we tackle conviction. For the moment, the leader's role in ensuring stability yet striving for flexibility brings us back to adventure and experimentation. If you can hardwire the corporation to accept and to react to the unpredictable, then you have significantly enhanced the firm's sustained capacity to find a point of differentiation that isn't different for the sake of being different but is different because customers value the difference.

The alternative is to be ordinary – yourself and your organization – to value passivity and cosiness. Alex Trotman of Ford speaks candidly of the perils:

> Complacency and sitting still when I should have been moving – that's where my biggest mistakes have been made.

How little we foresee the consequences either of wise or
unwise action, of virtue or of malice. Without this measureless
and perpetual uncertainty the drama of human life would be
destroyed.

Winston Churchill
The Second World War (vol 1) 1948

Taking the Organization by Surprise

Ian Preston of Scottish Power has a reputation for being a 'hard
man' – words like autocratic and explosive spring to mind. He is
inclined to barge into the offices of his senior team-members and
say of ideas and documents, 'I don't like this!'. He admits, 'I have
been known to tear documents to shreds. Sometimes I regret this
but I don't have time to fuss.' He prefers the epithet 'uncompromising' but let's not quibble; he told me he was secretly pleased
with the reputation. Why? After all, he works hard to build trust
and friendly relationships and demonstrates in everything he does
his commitment to the interests of the company and the people
in it. His explanation is insightful:

> Although I never do it deliberately, at times my angry sessions
> disturb the equilibrium and this helps me to learn more about
> people and situations.

This can be accomplished another way by constantly shifting
responsibility down to other managers – giving your job away, if
you like – so that others are confronted in an ongoing way by
greater and greater challenges. Peter Ellwood at TSB says, 'I ask
lots of tough questions of managers: it makes people re-think
assumptions and pre-empts complacency.' Leaders who do this,
of course, also free themselves for more complex strategic thinking or new directions.

In the January–February (1995) edition of *Harvard Business
Review*, Sumantra Ghoshal and Christopher Bartlett positively
advocate disruption:

> To facilitate the renewal process, top managers must take on a new
> role – one that disturbs the organizational equilibrium. We are not
> suggesting that top managers' job is to create chaos. Their role as
> shapers of corporate purpose still means they must provide direc-

tion and coherence. But we are saying that top managers must also direct some of their energy into more disruptive pursuits. (p.94)

At the organizational level, Bill Cockburn upsets the applecart in a deliberate way. He emphasizes the need to identify 'the moment to take staff by surprise to achieve a big surge.' His use of the word 'surprise' is precise; he is aiming to excite, to grab attention, even to shock. Once again, this seems to contradict the importance of communicating to staff, keeping them informed and onside. But, again, leadership is concerned with contradiction. People need information, but they also need a jolt to get them to take the first step to change. 'A few years ago,' says Derek Wanless at NatWest, 'in the retail bank, it is true that we needed to create uncertainty. Using shock tactics is legitimate when there is inertia in a business. The movement away from the traditional banking notion of a job for life is one example of that. But we're pretty well through that. I want structural stability now.'

At the same time, when unpredictability has delivered the momentum for change, people need to be excited by new horizons, to be inspired. Shock must be balanced by the opportunity for individuals to *do* more or *be* more. Textbooks on organizational behaviour often include a chapter on communication, with neat diagrams setting out the information source, the receiver, sources of noise and so forth. Sage advice covers specificity, clarity, timeliness and feedback. But this is like describing an organization purely in terms of the balance sheet or process flows. A huge chunk of communication, especially when it comes from leaders, must be about emotion, the way it makes people feel. That need not necessarily mean feeling good. Some leaders are obnoxious, intimidating, and unpredictable. They are capable of driving people to both lows and highs. Still, they attract talented people who want to work for them. Paul Carroll in *Big Blues* (1993) describes Lou Gerstner when he was at American Express:

> Through the closed door of his office, he might be heard yelling, 'That's the stupidest thing I've ever heard! You're an idiot! Get out of my office!'. If those in the hall hung around a second, they'd see some red-faced employee shoot out the door ... . One subordinate says that knees literally buckled and hands trembled when Gerstner walked into a room. (p.352)

Inspiration takes continuous effort, not just big spurts. We are inclined to mistake the great oratory of some leaders, Churchill for example, as the essence of leadership. We shall fight on the beaches, and all that. Yes, big events count. In business, there's no denying that the big initiatives are the things to plan and organize with a fine toothed comb. For the rest, at the individual level, the creation of unpredictability in managers' daily work raises the stakes, delivers challenge and distils the best from their talent. If you're the leader of a senior team, it is important to understand that one of the most critical factors contributing to your business unit or company's success and your personal success is how talented a team of people you can bring together and regularly *rearrange*. Comfort, ease, complacency, sitting still – these are the enemies of the top team. The key in the future will be continually to rearrange top teams in order to drive change.

Often this can mean bringing in several senior people from outside. 'I've tried to get people into the team from different backgrounds,' says Derek Wanless. 'In the past succession came through the retail bank. For a number of years that's no longer been acceptable in a Group like this with a portfolio of businesses. Now we have a range of skills.'

Bill Cockburn wants to see this in the management development practices of The Post Office. 'We need to create commercial acumen,' he says, 'in an organization that traditionally hasn't required it. Since we have many business and management units, we can develop some managers by cross-business moves.'

It can be immensely difficult to move people around an organization. I have had hours of frustrating debate in companies with executives who, on the one hand, know that rearranging people in senior roles is a good idea but who on the other hand, present every objection in the book for why it won't work in that particular outfit: we need specialists; it takes time to get to grips with a senior job; individuals will resist a step into the unknown; their bosses will refuse to part with trusted talent; no one will want to make the first move that might set the ball rolling. The list goes on. In practice, given a strong steer by the CEO and the top team, such objections always turn out to be overblown. All it takes is the first nudge (the act of leadership, in fact). By contrast, in the absence of cross-business movement, managerial jobs (and their incumbents) ossify. For the twenty-first century, that's corporate suicide.

The Unpredictable Icon

He is mobbed wherever he goes. People want to touch him. Schoolchildren happily line up to give him their pocket money, women fling their jewellery at him, small traders and business-men have raised billions of rupees for his cause. His rallies get bigger and more stirring by the day. Rousing slogans proclaim him as the next prime minister of Pakistan.

He is Imran Khan, a former captain of Pakistan's cricket team, who shot to glory after Pakistan won cricket's World Cup in 1992. These days Mr Khan is raising money for a cancer hospital for the poor in memory of his mother, who died of the disease. More worryingly for Pakistan's political leaders, the prime minister Benazir Bhutto, and the opposition's Nawaz Sharif, he has become a popular icon.

Until recently, the Oxford-educated Mr Khan wore Armani suits, dated London socialites and rubbed shoulders with rock stars. Now he has turned his back on all that. Clad in traditional Pakistani *shalwar kameez*, he claims the West is immoral, depraved, hypocritical and imperialistic. He accuses Pakistani ruling elites of being heartless and corrupt. There is talk of forming a welfare party or pressure group to address the plight of the 'wretched of the earth'.

To Pakistanis the new Imran Khan is noble (he comes from a noble line of Pathans), truthful (he admitted that he had once 'tampered' with the ball in a county cricket match), selfless (cancer hospital for the poor), independent (he is critical of all politicians and parties) and homespun (he refuses to wear western clothes and frowns on western music). He scolds upper-class children for aspiring to become 'brown sahibs'. He insists that his hospital will not become dependent on handouts from the rich and powerful. His populist rhetoric evokes standing ovations across the country...

The economy is slack. For the third year running, growth is expected to be lower than the 6% average for the 1980s. Many industries, including cotton (the country's top foreign-exchange earner) and sugar, are in bad shape. Since March [1994], the Karachi Stock Exchange index has declined 727 points to 1936 in December.

The country is steadily drifting into a pro-Islam, anti-West mood. Pakistanis felt betrayed when the United States, a staunch ally for over four decades, cut off economic and military aid in 1990 in retaliation for Pakistan's refusal to abandon its nuclear programme. Lack of western support for the cause of Muslims in Kashmir and Bosnia is seen as part of the West's 'new crusade against Islam'.

In this atmosphere of despair and drift many people find themselves yearning for a saviour to provide security, stability and self-respect. Can the born-again Muslim Imran Khan take on this role? For the moment, Mr Khan is insisting that he is not interested in politics because he finds it 'contemptible'.

The Economist, 'Pakistan's mighty Khan'
(7–13 January 1995, p.54).
© *The Economist*, January 1995.
Reprinted by special permission.

Taking the Market (and the Competition) by Surprise

If you don't get it, it'll get you, might be the watchword of business leaders for the twenty-first century. The world changes so rapidly today. We only have to look around us to see companies that believed they were untouchable, whose business processes and systems were as good as anyone else's and which they therefore didn't attempt to adjust. Now they are having to respond to the challenges. The world changes every day. Enormous organizations like AT&T and Hewlett Packard are trying to make themselves more like small businesses, reacting faster to customers, driving decision-making down as low as possible, reorganizing on a team and product basis, and generally attempting to become more entrepreneurial, to be as nimble as their smaller rivals in constantly anticipating market changes.

'We are here,' says Derek Wanless of NatWest's senior team, 'to think the unthinkable. Would the Group be better off broken up? Could the businesses operate better separately than under the Group banner? At the moment I think we are vastly better off together, but that doesn't stop us thinking about completely different scenarios.'

Constantly anticipating the market, the competition, trends in the business community, the future – this is a leadership role. Simon Dyer, Director General of the Automobile Association, agrees:

I spend a good deal of my time thinking about changes in the future market. Some of that is extrapolation from current trends, for instance the implications of motor manufacturers offering for free some of the services that we sell, but also more radical ideas that are entirely unknown to customers as yet – in-car technology such as navigation, for example. We also look carefully at the range of business options open to us, like possible joint ventures … . I want to make sure we find our niche.

Constant self-examination, searching the market and scanning the future to ensure that your firm remains competitive is the job of the senior team. It is concerned with anticipating future needs in relation to current practice and then articulating the required change. It boils down to the question: What is the future going to hold? One of the practical ways of answering this question is to benchmark, to search in an ongoing way for best practices that produce world class quality. The comparison need not be with competitors. Many of the best benchmark companies are outside your own industry, but share similar functions, processes and methods. Apple Computer, for example, has been used by many firms, from entirely different backgrounds, as a role-model for product development.

Apple is not the company it once was. Over a period of two months to July 1993 its share price had slumped 50 per cent and, to regain lost ground, CEO Michael Spindler has slashed operating and production costs and is launching a full-scale assault on the two dominant players in the vast PC market, Intel and Microsoft. Despite these problems, Apple is still seen as one of the leaders in product innovation. For business leaders this is the crucial point. The lessons of excellence in product innovation and development can be applied just the same in whatever your business is, as in hi-tech industries. However, the challenge is never-ending. There is always a gap between where you are and where you need to be. As you try to leap the gap, you can be pretty sure it's widening again.

Some executives would despair or merely plod on in the hope of miracles. Others wouldn't take the risk of changing anything substantial in the organization. After all, poking around and rearranging the innards of large corporations is messy, time-consuming and stressful. But a leadership team must look at the necessity to change critically and objectively, as was the case at Chrysler in the early 1980s. Huge organizations like Chrysler and Sony are striving to develop the ability to outperform their

competitive set and transform themselves faster than the competition.

Alex Trotman is prepared to go a step further. He insists, 'Fix
it when it ain't broken', and he's serious. He wants to institution-
alize change and the change process in Ford. This means looking
outward, at the market and competitors, all the time. 'Benchmark
the daylights out of best practice,' he contends. 'Know your
customer absolutely like your brother or your sister. Aim to
exceed your customer expectations, not just meet them ... . And
when you've done all that, be dissatisfied, because if you beat the
best benchmark company, it isn't going to be sitting still while you
go to beat it. And if you exceed your customer's expectations, the
customer isn't sitting still because ten years from now they'll have
higher expectations.'

I call this 'taking the market by surprise' – continuously being
ahead of the game, beyond expectations, beyond the analysis and
prediction of competitors. It is virtually, but not quite, impossible
to achieve, but even the striving after it makes the difference to
an organization, gives the best business leaders, in their field, the
edge. Trotman goes further: 'We're a very successful company.
We're building on strength. We're determined to build on
strength while we're strong.' Leaving it until you're in trouble (or
nearly so) lands you in the predicament of having to catch up
before you can get ahead – an impossible situation. Blindingly
obvious, I concede, but it is surprising how many CEOs, with the
wherewithal to do something about it, permit organizational drift,
turned to stone by internal politics, or talking about problems a
lot but always tackling them a day late.

That's the worst case (and regrettably the most common). The
best is nicely encapsulated by Hamel and Prahalad in *Competing
for the Future*: 'The goal is not simply to be led by customers'
expressed needs; responsiveness is not enough. The objective is
to amaze customers by anticipating and fulfilling their unarticu-
lated needs.' (p 291)

Giving up the Past to Operate in the Future

Here's another contradiction; ignore the past, I said in Chapter
3, at your peril. The opposite is also true; give up the past to
operate in the future. Business leaders have to do both. How do
we reconcile the two? Bill Cockburn states the case succinctly:

'Look at your history to understand what is valuable, then build on that for commercial value. Don't become obsessed with the past.' History is a means of imposing context, particularly in its reinterpretation – remember Alex Trotman's role as 'messenger from the past'.

At the same time, however, business leaders must eliminate all their former frames of reference in asking the question, 'What's the future going to look like?'. They must give up the past in order to operate in the future. This needs to happen at two levels – the personal and the organizational.

Let's take the personal level first. CEOs often fail, as we shall see later, because they are overly committed to the style and strategies that worked for them throughout their career. Understandable, but at the top, in a senior leadership position, this is not enough. What made you successful in your last job is not going to make you successful in a more senior leadership role. If you are under that illusion, you are very likely to fail. More about this anon.

For the moment, it is important to understand that the mind-set of being fixed on one way of doing things – at the personal level – carries over into the leadership of a firm, which is where the problems for the firm start. It is one thing to believe and invest wholeheartedly in a series of tactics (benchmarking, quality, brand creation, etc.) and thereby continuously take the market by surprise. It is quite another to make what Alex Trotman calls 'leaps ahead' – to build competitive advantage not from continuous change but quantum change. Business process re-engineering aspires to this. Leadership makes it happen. Trotman again:

> You have to do much better than that. So you have to then think about uncharted territory, then as a leader lead a team into uncharted territory, perhaps with a target that isn't exactly clear but lead the team to excellence beyond the level of excellence that you can find in benchmarking or in the present customers' satisfaction desires.

Uncharted territory, by its nature, is, well, uncharted. Finding both the right route and the right destination in *terra incognita* doesn't come from sitting and thinking about it. Hans Boom puts it this way: 'Sure I use project planning and time-plans, but I use them as maps to look for *other* ways to get to the destination. One thing you can be sure about project plans is they never work out as planned – but this doesn't mean you shouldn't have a plan!'

Trust a professional project planner to see through the allure of
all those neat lines and milestones on a page, their siren call telling
you that the plan *is* the journey.

Leaders look for other ways to get there. They're not satisfied
with the plan. They know the plan is there to be changed, that it
will be changed, most probably by circumstance but better still by
the visible hand of leadership. This includes changing the destination, not willy nilly but on the judgement of the leaders of a
business. 'You have to make leaps ahead,' says Trotman. 'Sometimes that comes from my head, sometimes from other heads in
that team. A non-conforming change from what *is* into something
very different – those kind of changes, strategic changes, come
from a few heads in the corporation.'

No matter the magnitude of risk or the difficulty in answering
the most searching of strategic questions, non-conforming
changes must be faced and addressed and decisions taken. The
leaders who shrink from this will fail or, like old soldiers, fade
away. Better that such risks are faced when a business is strong.
Better that leaders accept the impossibility of predicting the future
– gather their data, certainly, but speculate nonetheless – and
commit to a course of action. Trotman wants to develop new
markets, specifically China. How the Chinese will react is anybody's guess. 'This is one of the most difficult strategic questions
to answer,' he admits. 'Answer it we must. We must make
assumptions about how to answer that question, because it will,
in large part, determine our investment strategy, our Asia strategy,
perhaps partly our global strategy.'

Chaos, Predictability and the Butterfly Effect

[The] situation in the social sciences is not fundamentally
different from the situation in the physical sciences. It has long
been recognized that the laws of physics do not allow us to
predict with much certainty where any particular leaf from a
tree will fall. More recently, physical scientists have begun to
recognize the limits of predictability in a variety of systems,
such as ecological systems and weather systems. Although
some effects are robust and highly predictable, others are
extremely unstable. The term 'butterfly effect' has been coined
to describe small, unanticipatable perturbations that can have
dramatic effects (Gleick, 1987). The whimsical name refers to
a meteorologist's comment that a butterfly beating its wings

in Beijing can, under the right circumstances, have a detectable effect on the weather in the midwestern United States a few days later. As a consequence of the extreme sensitivity of weather to local perturbations, long-range weather forecasting not only is not possible now but also, according to some scientists, will never be possible.

Again, there is a question as to whether such effects can ever be predicted with precision in highly complex, interactive, nonlinear systems. But the discovery and description of the sources of such inherent unpredictability, whether in the physical sciences or the behavioral sciences, is hardly a cause for apology. It is an important intellectual contribution with profound theoretical and practical implications.

Ross & Nisbett
The Person and the Situation (1991, p.18)

The business world is complex. Small things have big effects. And, to extend Ross & Nisbett's argument to the business world, no corporate war-room is ever going to be able to accurately predict the success of this master strategy versus that one, or be entirely satisfied of the wisdom of launching one product over another – no matter how sophisticated the analysis or the forecasting capacities. Apart from anything else business leaders invariably use informal sources of data – tips, rumours, networks into competitors, and of course gut-feel about the future – rather than just the formal processes. And they're right to do so.

Tinkering, testing, piloting, experimenting – these are the strategic tools of the twenty-first century. For leaders the lessons are clear. You *cannot* control the future; executives at IBM long thought the future was theirs. You can't really predict it; but you can experiment; you can flex the business; you can rearrange management teams. Remember, leaving things as they are can be just as unpredictable as changing everything. You lose (or win) both ways.

SUMMARY

Unpredictability

1 *Adventure*: experiment. Induce crises. Don't sit still.

2 *Take the organization by surprise*: disturb the equilibrium. Give your job away. Rearrange the team.

3 *Take the market (and competition) by surprise*: benchmark best practice. Fix it when it isn't broken.

4 *Give up the past to operate in the future*: think about uncharted territory. Make leaps ahead. Answer the tough strategic questions.

6

CONVICTION

Corporate Pragmatism or Corporate Inspiration?

'You have to have a value set,' says Banc One CEO John McCoy. 'Everything that we do ties back to those values and to the brand.' Joseph Badaracco and Richard Ellsworth make a similar point in their book *Leadership and the Quest for Integrity* (1989):

> Leadership in a world of dilemmas is not, fundamentally, a matter of style, charisma, or professional management technique. It is a difficult daily quest for integrity. Managers' behavior should be an unadorned, consistent reflection of what they believe and what they aspire to for a company. Managers who take this approach earn trust. Commitment to leadership through integrity can help managers through the inevitable periods of anxiety, doubt, and trial, and give them a sense of priorities to guide them through an uncertain world. (p 209)

The point is well made and takes us back to my earlier comments in Chapter 2. Leadership cannot be 'taught' in a two week training course. It is impossible to teach conviction. How many people have the deep-rooted belief in the value of what they are doing and can communicate it to others so that they will follow? How many leaders, business, political or otherwise, can you identify and honestly say they are 'guided by faith and matchless fortitude' as John Milton declared of Oliver Cromwell? The opposite seems true. In December 1994 James Walsh, introducing *Time*'s global 100 leaders of the future, bemoaned the sad reality 'that politics has drifted into manipulation of people by 10-second sound-bite answers, rather than understanding of how the world really works and articulating some wisdom about it.' (5 December 1994, p 25) A line from W B Yeats' *The Second Coming* captures the essence of political leadership today:

> The best lack all conviction, while the worst
> are full of passionate intensity.

Ten-second sound-bites do not lead people for long. The artificial and the forced, no matter how artfully contrived, are veils through which most people will eventually see. And so, at heart, leadership does require adherence to a set of values or beliefs. Strong belief is inspirational. The belief in a leader is a kind of faith and faith can move mountains.

In business, however, it is almost always difficult to articulate something more than mere corporate pragmatism. But when an organization is perceived as simply in the business of business and nothing more, and employees are simply employed, what is there for its members to get hold of? What does it mean to work each day? Is it to provide a good return to shareholders? Is it really just to 'make a living'? During the preceding chapters we have dealt with some of the elements of leadership that do make a difference: the imposition of context or meaning for the people who make up the organization; the creation of risk and opportunity to draw from people not just the hard effort of workaday grind, but daring and imagination; and lastly, the disturbance of equilibrium and predictability to jolt people out of an acceptance of the ordinary.

A Shadow of Doubt

> Our doubts are traitors,
> And make us lose the good we oft might win,
> By fearing to attempt.
>
> William Shakespeare
> Lucio in *Measure for Measure*

Belief in Self

'You should stand on your own – have an opinion and be able to defend it,' asserts Ian Preston at Scottish Power. 'The worst position for a leader to get into is to be seen simply as the vehicle of his management's opinions or the Board's opinions.' When the business is in difficulties or the financial markets express their dissatisfaction with the latest results and it seems impossible to get the message across publicly that your strategy for the business in the medium and longer term is the right one, then is the time when conviction counts. At some level business leaders have to believe in their heart of hearts that they're doing the right thing.

I asked the same question of Hans Boom apropos the go-stop-go progress of the Betuweroute following a change of government in The Netherlands: did he have doubts that it would ever go ahead? 'I have to be convinced,' he replied, 'that the railway will come – whether in 1998 or 2008. I have to believe that. You can't fake it! If I started to doubt the feasibility, quite apart from the impact on my team, I would have to resign immediately.'

No matter the size of the initiative or decision, its impact, cost or risk, much of its success will hinge not on whole volumes of analysis or risk management or intricate commercial alliances, but on the conviction of a business leader. On Ford's globalization strategy, which over the next few years will absorb tens of billions of dollars, ultimately the driving force behind it is, in Alex Trotman's words, that 'you believe it'. A hundred corporate analysts armed with every conceivable set of statistics might argue for its brilliance or its folly – only the deepest conviction will make it happen.

John Clark regards himself as a professional chief executive. He has transformed a number of businesses and for the past four years has been reorganizing and rebuilding BET. Leading this corporate transformation in the initial stages required little short of total self-belief. 'Let nothing get in your way,' says Clark. 'Making the first phase work – the reorganization and cost reduction – needed very strong personal leadership, making personal sacrifices, working seven days a week, but at the same time showing clearly to the organization that what was rewarded now was running a business that generates cash not a paper-profit.'

Self-belief is important at a number of levels. First, it invests leaders with authority. Never pretend that authority comes with the title. Ian Preston's warning about becoming merely a vehicle of management or board opinion is a warning about the loss of credibility and the authority that goes with it. Second, the pure belief in the importance and value of a goal or enterprise acts as a target for everyone else. It focuses energy that might otherwise become diffuse or wastefully channelled into organizational politics. 'A CEO needs to wipe out politics,' declares John Clark. 'When you have too many people with not enough to do, then you end up with bad politics. I keep people in different patches so busy they don't have time for politics.'

A third reason for the importance of self-belief is one we touched on in Chapter 5 – what Derek Wanless calls 'absorbing uncertainty'. For individuals to believe that a specific strategy is the right one, or a tough decision cannot be reversed, or the pain of an initiative must be borne in the longer term interest, the behaviour of leaders is all-important. We look to leaders, at the very least for confirmation of our beliefs, sometimes even – in religion and politics especially – for the affirmation of what we should believe, but more often to convince us that day-to-day uncertainties or misfortunes need not distract or divert us from the objectives of real importance.

How leaders accomplish this can seem deceptively simple. What does Derek Wanless mean by 'absorbing uncertainty'? He replies with a laugh; 'Appearing more confident than you are!'

Bill Cockburn talks in a similar vein; 'I am being looked at all the time. If I looked worried, they'd be worried.'

It is not as simple as it sounds. The pressure to shift from a course of action raises doubts. Doubts undermine action and are easy to sense. Moments of hesitation lose the initiative. In the face of doubt, courage is all that counts. Courage, of course, is a word little used in business in the 1990s; the dry formality of management technique has found higher favour. And yet courage has always had a place, though we might not choose to discuss it or reward it. Every leader who deals with the bad news and does something about it – rather than avoiding it or concealing it – shows courage.

How Much More can we Take?

On Tuesday 18 May 1982, the British War Cabinet met and authorized a land attack on the Falklands Islands to drive out the Argentinian occupying forces. Margaret Thatcher, then Prime Minister, related her doubts and anxiety as the initial phase of the attack progressed:

> At Northwood I spent some time getting up to date in the Operations Room. I did my best to seem confident, but when I left with Admiral Fieldhouse and we were out of earshot of anyone else, I could not help asking him: 'how long can we go on taking this kind of punishment?' He was no less worried. But he also had the ability of a great commander to see the other side of things. And, terrible as our losses had been and would

be in the future, the fact was that we had landed our forces successfully and that serious losses were being inflicted on the Argentine airforce.

Margaret Thatcher
The Downing Street Years (1993, p226)

Ubuntu ... Humaneness, Trust

Junior Potloane at Nedcor Bank describes an African concept – 'ubuntu' – which translates roughly from the Sotho language as, 'A person is a person through other people'. When we are separated by cultures it is tempting in business to dismiss such concepts as alien and irrelevant. Hold on a moment. Potloane goes on to talk about the implications for business and leadership:

> One of my principles is that I'll say of you in your absence what I'll say to your face. Being open and frank helps enormously in developing working relationships, particularly when it comes to managing diversity in South Africa.

The element of trust between Black and White is not one that exists intact in South African businesses. Nevertheless, a great deal of effort has now gone into building bridges between cultures and, although the situation is accentuated in South Africa, the need to build trust in working relationships is just as important for leaders elsewhere in the world. Dave Bowyer at Megapak:

> The team you inherit may not trust you because of a predecessor's history and way of doing things. Also, mistrust between Black and White is still high. My job is to be *consistent*. The managing director is one of the people and I have to treat everyone with the same trust. People trust me because I trust them, but if they let me down...

In short, the position is clear. Managers and staff know where they stand. There is trust. 'You have to be very much driven,' agrees Alex Trotman, 'by the basic belief that it's people that make the whole thing work, and that without that belief you're not really going to be successful.' This requires consistency or integrity in relationships: there are things I can agree to and things I cannot; there are things I will expect and things you can expect; we shall both live up to our expectations of each other. Hans Boom brings this alive in his own colourful way:

To give one simple example, I'm always determined to be on time – both personally and in terms of projects. Likewise, if I'm expecting someone and they're late, after 15 minutes I won't receive them anymore. This gives you a reputation for *delivering*.

Many people in organizations do not deliver on time. Being an exception creates both expectation and trust, both within the business and outside it. And so conviction requires that leaders live and breathe a code of conduct, which can be implicit – as long as it models the kind of behaviour that you want to see lower down the organization. In some firms for example I have seen an explicit code of conduct introduced for the top team and then cascaded throughout the business. Its objective is to provide a set of standards and rules about how people deal with each other. The example given below is a code of conduct merged from several such codes developed for senior teams.

Code of Conduct for Executive Team

1 Dedication to customer service will underpin everything that senior executives do.

2 Senior executives will make time for the senior team and each other.

3 In their own actions and words, senior executives will make clear their support of managers and staff throughout the firm.

4 Senior executives will be mutually supportive and will accept and demonstrate joint responsibility for each other's actions.

5 Senior executives will give and accept open criticism.

6 Where there are disputes or issues unresolved, the senior executives involved will:

   – agree to communicate
   – declare the purpose of the discussion
   – each put forward his or her point of view
   – reflect the other's point of view
   – agree a way forward

7 Documents will be circulated at least 48 hours before meetings.

---

8   All executives will prepare fully for meetings.

9   In meetings, executives will adhere to the set end time.

10 In meetings or interactions executives will remain objective and attempt to signal emotion before outbursts occur.

One of the most common reasons for the failure of leaders arriving new at the head of a team – whether the failure amounts to delay in effecting change or being removed because of non-performance – is the inability to build trust. With trust comes wholehearted support and the willingness to commit greater effort than usual to the leader's agenda. The flip-side brings not just disgruntled apathy but what amounts to passive, sometimes even active, sabotage. I can recall cases in organizations where the atmosphere of distrust in the senior management group was so thick an outsider could almost touch it. To insiders the word 'distrust' was seldom used but a culture of blame and defensiveness would often be manifest in 'us and them' statements; the bounds of accountability would be blurred; and the atmosphere cascaded inevitably downwards to infect the operation of the rest of the business.

Leaders feel helpless in these circumstances. Despite the best of intentions, making anything happen is like walking in treacle. Pounding the desk produces frenetic action – more so than usual – but no results. Tightening command and control offers the illusion of clarity and stability, yet events seem to spiral ever faster out of reach. Even sudden and dramatic changes in style, from threats to cajoling and gentle persuasion, offer, at best, only a momentary respite, at worst, a fatal loss of credibility. This is when desperation can be measured by countless 'vital' but failed projects that had been intended to sort things out. Finally, there comes a point when it is too late for a new leader to retrieve the situation – when the management team have implicitly accepted and unconsciously conspire in their leader's downfall.

Up until that point, trust can still be rebuilt, even if it necessitates the replacement of some of the more recalcitrant members of the management team. A few years ago one CEO summed up the situation to me like this: 'One or two of the old top team objected to my style. They've gone.' In other words, at some point, leaders *must* take uncomfortable decisions, for the organization's sake and their own survival, but they can only do this when they have imposed with absolute clarity the context for the business: 'This is what we are in the business of doing. We haven't got it right thus far. But in the future these are the things that will matter … . You are either with me, or you must go.' Alex Watson of Chep in Europe speaks of exactly this in relation to his own experience:

> When you are imposed on an existing team as its leader, it takes time to express to people what your vision is and what changes may occur, and equally that, until proven wrong, everyone is staying but some in time, realistically, will not be here … .

'Firing people. Yes, it has to be done sometimes,' concedes John Clark. 'I don't like it, but it is necessary. First you have to try the right management techniques to make the situation work, but when it comes down to it and you fire someone, in most circumstances the people around recognize that the change was necessary and that it enables you to go forward again.' All too often the context becomes blurred during the preceding struggle to get the basic work done. In short, leaders drift into doing nothing other than *managing*; they are too embroiled to lift either their own sights or anyone else's. Worse still, they have no relationship of trust upon which to build action and results.

'Ensuring the company is heading in the right direction is one of the key tasks of leadership,' says Nelson Robertson of General Accident, but adds, 'The means of doing this is exercised through relationships. I'm *not* saying leadership is about shaking hands with 17,000 people in the company every year, but you do need to *know* people in your wider team and ensure they know what *you* want, eventually without almost needing to ask you … . You need to trust people by building relationships.'

If all this sounds weak and woolly and hardly the stuff of the tough management and corporate heroism to which you aspire, take note of Robertson's next comment, made almost in the same breath:

> I usually hammer people who say they've got the best team in the company. Their perspective is limited. They have to realize that they are part of a larger team, beyond their own immediate area, with different requirements, but which they have to satisfy as well. These people are often the ones who struggle with working upwards and providing the performance necessary to bring effectiveness to their wider team – my team.

Building trust, then, is hard work for leaders. It embraces multiple relationships across and down the business and, for leaders of business units, upwards as well. Although Robertson, like his peers in any other firm, has enormous pressure on his time he still makes the point, 'I have to make sufficient opportunities to build relationships; whether it's as simple as lunch with my management team or overseas visits, all these opportunities force us together more.'

Simon Dyer, Director General of the Automobile Association, reflects on the same issue:

> Unfortunately it all takes time. It makes the problem of keeping your finger on the pulse and maintaining relationships very difficult. But it has to be done. I keep constant contact on the ground with people all over the UK, visiting branch offices, getting around head office, the patrols on the road ... and in various parts of the world in my international role.

The result is critical to personal and organizational success. Even Ian Preston, who concedes that he is tough and uncompromising with his managers, emphasizes the value of trust: 'People will do what you want without your having to make them, when they trust you, respect you and respect your commitment to the well-being of the company.' In the extreme, when circumstances are at their most pressing, trust is all a leader can rely on. Ian Preston goes on, 'People should be able to read me well enough to know that when I impose by edict something on staff, they can go along with it completely, because I have sound, logical reasons which are in the interest of the company as a whole – even if the reasons aren't transparent. Why do they go along with me? Because I've treated them fairly in the past.'

In the end, what trust comes down to is best expressed by Peter Ellwood at TSB:

> We must make sure that we, as a senior management team, care about people, that we have a set of values about how we deal with people: respect, integrity and openness.

You Can Rely on Me

A small but growing body of psychological research underlines the contention that trust is fundamental to leadership effectiveness. A number of discrete patterns of behaviour seems to matter most in building trust, notably:

- sharing appropriate information;
- willingness to be influenced;
- not abusing subordinates' vulnerability;
- fairness, in relation to the value of subordinates' contributions; and
- fulfilling promises.

In short, trust is the expectancy of subordinates that they can rely on the word of a leader.

See Kouzes and Posner (1987), Rotter (1967) and Zand (1972)

Telling it Like it is

In leadership positions there is, perhaps, only one thing harder than knowing how and when to face problems, or come clean, or tell it like it really is – and that's *doing* it. 'To walk away from the uncomfortable decisions,' Alex Watson acknowledges, 'simply causes problems – lack of respect, for a start. I have to have an element of respect and therefore I can't fudge decisions on colleagues who need to be put right.'

Ian Preston has a maxim he likes to quote: 'You undervalue your best by being soft on your worst. You must reward the excellent people and give nothing to the non-performers. There must be a clear distinction.'

Both of these comments reflect the virtue (not infrequently absent in many top managers) of tackling the issues that are hardest to face. We would all much rather deal with the exciting and the enjoyable, leaving unpleasant business to someone else – delegating it even. The same applies to the type of information we value. Passed up through the internal circuitry of the organization, via all manner of filters and processors, information on the market, competitors and results can be irretrievably distorted. Middle management and poor IT are not the only offenders. A leader's nearest and dearest colleagues can be 'encouraged' to present only the good news, or bad news in a positive light. Some years ago, when I was talking to the CEO of a large multinational about this, he used a phrase which I think puts the matter beyond contention:

> With all the unabating pressure, uncertainty and complexity of
> working at board level, I think it dawned on me eventually that
> there is real value in no-shit honesty in whatever you're doing.

The same is true when the audience is a much larger one. 'Change
is an unsettling business,' says Peter Ellwood of TSB. 'It is vital
that even when the message is a bitter blow to those who receive
it, they must know as soon as possible. It should be communicated
clearly, energetically and honestly.'

Leaders create problems for themselves by doing the opposite,
by skirting around the nub of a problem – either because of politics
(someone important might be upset) or fear ('can it really be that
bad?') or squeamishness ('let's pretend everything's okay'). It's
true, of course, that the mantle of leadership authority comes with
the double-edged sword of followers' compliance; most people
automatically oblige you in what they believe you want to hear
rather than what you should be told. Moreover, what they believe
you should hear oddly coincides with what suits them best to tell
you. There is a self-serving transaction here that is no more than
human nature, but terribly dangerous for any leader. We might
call it the 'Thatcher syndrome'. I speculate (as, I'm sure, have
many others) that Margaret Thatcher's strong, decisive approach
as the leader of the Conservative party in Britain produced a
milieu within the cabinet and among her advisors of too-ready
acceptance of the verity of what Thatcher herself held as unques-
tioned articles of faith. In short, the mechanism for giving honest
feedback failed. The Prime Minister was largely isolated, seeing
only what she wanted to see. She might not have wanted it that
way, but it was what she got. In a sense she created her own
downfall by engendering the conditions in which her closest
colleagues would be unable to present her with accurate information. Truth had long since become a casualty. When it became
apparent at the eleventh hour, it was too late. 'I was sick at heart,'
she discloses in her autobiography (1993). 'I could have resisted
the opposition of opponents and potential rivals and even respected
them for it; but what grieved me was the desertion of those I had
always considered friends and allies and the weasel words
whereby they had transmuted their betrayal into frank advice and
concern for my fate.' (p 855)

Any leader may face this. It is the risk you run of holding
convictions and occupying a position that too readily becomes
insulated against bad news and free from healthy challenge. Utter
belief produces unsurpassed collective will among a leader's

followers. But when conviction threatens to cloud the rarefied heights a leader occupies, it is useless to pretend that you can see clear sky; the only security is a blast of cold reality – the sooner the better.

'It's fine to be self-confident,' concurs Peter Ellwood. 'That will come from your track-record. But you also must have what I call "commercial humility"; constantly questioning yourself. After all, your knowledge out of the total of knowledge, even just in the business world, is tiny. So you are confronted perpetually with the difficult combination of needing to be confident in the face of problems and humble in the light of your own ignorance.'

'When you don't have a firm view,' declares Robert van Gelder at Boskalis, 'you should tell people this: "Our position is unclear. There are different arguments for and against and I don't know yet. What do *you* think?" In this way you get closer to the answers.'

Doing this is a risk and has to be judged as such, but the courage of honesty in difficult circumstances can make the difference between success and failure. It brings new facts and new options and, most important of all, halts the treadmill, prevents the inexorable rush along a course you have not chosen.

The Honest and the Unquestioningly Obedient

But far more numerous was the herd of such,
Who think too little, and who talk too much.

John Dryden
Absalom and Achitophel

If your Heart's not in it ... or if it is, but too Much

The trouble with conviction is that it is or it isn't, you have it or you don't. You can appear more confident than you are (for a time), as several leaders have attested in this chapter, but entering on a new strategy, reorganizing process linkages or investing substantially in the redesign of a suite of products requires sustained commitment and belief. That's hard enough in a stable environment. However, as we are all too aware, the world of business changes and different things are important at different times. How do leaders remain indefatigable in their convictions amidst so much change and uncertainty?

The answer to this is straightforward, if slightly surprising. Hans Boom probably sums it up the most neatly:

> Before I take on a job, I ask myself the questions: Is the work interesting? Do I like the people? Can I work with them? If any of the answers are 'no', then I won't take it on. Otherwise things can go badly wrong.

You might object that Boom is an independent, a consultant hired for a major infrastructure project. He can choose to take it on or withdraw. True – but the point is that leaders will only be at their best when they are interested in what they are doing, when they believe in it.

Ian Preston at Scottish Power claims 'I never had a job I didn't enjoy.' Derek Wanless of NatWest relates the story of how, in the early part of his career, his branch manager, Dennis Child, was hugely influential in getting him really interested in banking, particularly in terms of customer service. Robert van Gelder of Boskalis says, 'I want to carry this business further. It is the challenge of the business that I enjoy – not the personal ambition, but being a major force in the market and seeing things come to fruition, executing strategy.'

The implications of this for aspiring leaders are clear – don't take on roles as the leader of an enterprise merely for the status, the career prospects it brings or the money. If you don't believe in it, you won't succeed. Your heart won't be in it and you will always be tempted, under pressure, to take the easier option and not the right one, to cut and run. Why? Because your status, or your career or the money will always matter more than what is right for the business. Moreover, if your heart isn't in it, your colleagues will sense it. Why should they care if you don't? And so on down the line.

Quite often, what the organization stands for and what it is doing drift apart or, in the worst case, are entirely at odds. It is the job of leaders to understand this, to identify clearly what matters and to ensure that action aligns with context. Conviction will have nothing to do with hypocrisy and expedience. Conviction is concerned with winning the compelling argument, with determination, toughness and the relentless affirmation of 'a cause' or direction.

Still, we must not forget that conviction itself is only one among the elements that make up leadership. Out of balance with the others, its effect on leaders will be to encourage and entrench the autocratic and the authoritarian, to separate them from their followers, or to drive them to high risk ventures out of synchrony with the firm's need and future survival. These extremes of conviction produce around leaders a heroic and mythological aura impenetrable to even the closest colleagues and one that is ultimately destructive – personally and organizationally. It is for this reason that the senior management *team* is a crucial part of leadership effectiveness. Quite apart from their leadership responsibility over their own functional area and what each member brings to the diversity of capabilities of the top team in their professional knowledge of the business and (it is to be hoped, these days) other businesses, the senior group should be moulded by their leader into a team whose members work together to balance the authority, power and convictions of the most senior person – to act, as it were, as a reality check. The board of directors and independent or non-executive directors need to play a similar role, but all too frequently are inept – partly because the senior team want it that way (to avoid 'interference') and partly because board directors themselves have failed to understand and sensibly action this role.

The risks that can arise without an adequate reality check are not inconsiderable. It is sobering to reflect on the typical causes of company failures. Numbered among them are exposure brought about by overly complex financing arrangements, the difficulties of managing overseas investment, or poor control of financial transactions. Similarly, many companies have been left with excessive gearing and assets worth considerably less than they paid for them following over-enthusiastic expansion and acquisition on the back of easy access to finance. But one look at the list below (identified by Coopers & Lybrand's audit and insolvency teams) will tell you how often it is the case that weak board control is at fault in business failures:

- over-dominant and over-ambitious CEO or executive team;
- inadequate or biased information given to the board as a whole, infrequent board meetings or inadequate records of board decisions and reasoning;
- unbalanced boards in terms of the skills represented;

- strategies based on short-term share price rather than solidity of real earnings;
- inadequate systems of financial control, including weak or absent authorization procedures;
- failure to change policies in response to changing economic conditions; and
- unwillingness to admit to failure or bad news, leading into deeper difficulties (including failure to communicate with major lenders).

In Britain, problems like these led Sir Adrian Cadbury's committee on the financial aspects of corporate governance to recommend in 1992 that non-executive directors should take the lead in providing a strong, independent element on the board – especially where this relates to issues of strategy, performance, resources (including key appointments) and standards of conduct. In short, their involvement should carry weight on the board.

There is no doubt that many CEOs and their teams have mixed feelings about this. Is it a benefit, a limitation, a threat? This depends on whether leaders actively try to make the board work, considering not just the knowledge of the irritations and constraints that an effective board may bring, but also the dangers that its absence may produce. The extremes of conviction and the pressures of isolation to which leadership is prone should be reason enough.

Conviction on its own is the most powerful and the most dangerous of human characteristics. It is fanaticism. Once again it is worth remembering Friedrich Nietzsche's profound observation and warning:

Men believe in the truth of all that is seen to be strongly believed in.

The Achievement and Folly of Uncompromising Conviction

Henry Ford, starting with nothing in 1905, had fifteen years later built the world's largest and most profitable manufacturing enterprise. The Ford Motor Company, in the early twenties, dominated and almost monopolized the American automobile market and held a leadership position in most of the other important automobile markets of the world. In addition, it had amassed, out of profits, cash reserves of a billion dollars or so.

Yet only a few years later, by 1927, this seemingly impregnable business empire was in shambles. Having lost its leadership position and barely a poor third in the market, it lost money almost every year for twenty years or so, and remained unable to compete vigorously right through World War II. In 1944 the founder's grandson, Henry Ford II, then only twenty-six years old and without training or experience, took over, ousted two years later his grandfather's cronies in a palace coup, brought in a totally new management team and saved the company.

It is not commonly realized that this dramatic story is far more than a story of personal success and failure. It is, above all, what one might call a controlled experiment in mismanagement.

The first Ford failed because of his firm belief that a business did not need managers and management. All it needed, he believed, was the owner-entrepreneur with his 'helpers'. The only difference between Ford and most of his contemporaries in business was that, as in everything he did, Henry Ford stuck uncompromisingly to his convictions. He applied them strictly, firing or sidelining any one of his 'helpers', no matter how able, who dared to act as a 'manager', make a decision or take action without orders from Ford … .

Peter Drucker
Management (1977, pp307–308)

SUMMARY

Conviction

1 *Believe in yourself*: stand on your own. Have an opinion and be able to defend it. Be courageous.

2 *Trust*: actively build relationships. Listen. Share information. Be fair. Fulfil your promises.

3 *Tell it like it is*: face up to and tackle problems, especially people problems. Get your own regular reality check.

4 *Put your heart into it*: be determined, tough and relentless, but don't become a fanatic.

7

GENERATING CRITICAL MASS

... Or, Doing More Than Making Things Happen

While conviction produces unsurpassed collective will among a leader's followers, alone it cannot move people in the intended direction or along the most productive route. Conviction is catalytic – it causes action – but it is uncontrolled. It is easily dissipated in large organizations with conflicting internal and external demands, all the more so as change and complexity accelerate. The forces at work in modern organizations are immense. Expectations of employees have changed: they want to participate more, they want to have responsibility and make decisions, bring their intelligence to bear in their jobs and do more than just follow instructions. The nature of companies has changed too; it is no longer effective or efficient to have people in Box 1 executing a task, followed by people in Box 2, each box separated by a *cordon sanitaire*. Shifting market demands and competitive pressures mean that businesses have to bring together a lot of diverse elements internally – and a lot of diverse elements externally – to achieve any major impact in today's complex global economy.

Moreover, the traditional concepts that ruled management theory for decades (and are still practised by millions of managers) have begun to crumble. How you organize, how you manage, how you lead are no longer fixed. 'The classic pyramid command structure has been stripped away,' BET's John Clark declares. 'The General Motors model was the "control" model' – this is no longer tenable.' He's right. Vast new markets and trading blocs, global competition in a borderless world, the incessant pressure of rising customer service expectations, a wave of new technology and IT within and outside businesses – all these things have demanded faster decision-making, faster design, faster customer response times, faster production, not to mention the givens of innovation and quality. The old structures of organization and management, bureaucracy and control, hierarchy and accountability are under pressure. And so they should be.

Business schools and management books (including this one) are full of concepts such as the following:

- re-engineering;
- process simplification;
- corporate transformation;
- global marketing and strategy;
- business restructuring;
- managing change;
- chaos theory;
- Euromanagement(!).

Many managers mock what they see as new religions, here today, gone tomorrow. Perfectly true, in some cases. Fads do come and go – most make little real difference, often because they're aimed at the wrong bits of the organizational jigsaw or because the organizational jigsaw itself doesn't fit its environment. But all of these new management ideas and fads together tell us about the trend. Businesses need better solutions to difficult problems all the time. There is no let-up. The list above is simply another source of data for leaders about the problems and demands that (have hit!) will hit their firms next.

There is a tendency, though, to be blown along by this storm of new ideas to the point where, battered and bruised, all you can think about is doing what everyone else is doing, which, in effect, these days, is major change, big initiatives, giant leaps. Leadership, as discussed in Chapter 5, is not just about the big events. There is a day-to-day demand on leaders to make the right judgements, perhaps to decide *not* to launch the 'big restructuring' but to assess where best to place resource and effort. Should cost-reduction really be the top priority (despite every indication that this is so), or is the identification of new markets and the pursuit of revenue growth the only longer term strategy that will save the business? Judgement and risk (Chapter 4) are bound up together in such decisions, but they are not the only decisions that generate critical mass in an organization. There are small actions that are merely part of a chain but critical none the less – a quiet word here, an informal chat there, a decision to bring in outsiders or a manager's early promotion. Equally there are actions that sit somewhere between the big events and the day-to-day – producing the right organizational configurations or fronting a series of communications roadshows. Whatever the case, we are concerned here with the channelling of energy, not simply to produce individual action but to create in the organization *sufficient* charge or impetus to ensure that a state of critical mass is reached and sustained. I might have entitled this chapter 'Making things happen', but leadership does more than make things happen. It ensures that the effect of individual behaviour in an organization attains a point at which, cumulatively, something much larger than the sum total of individual action is contributed to the business.

Breaking it up, Breaking it down

'You haven't a hope of doing it to a large corporation,' a CEO flatly told me once. 'It's just not possible.' He was talking about major change, but behind that he's also dealing with the leadership of anything. When an organization gets so big (that is, complex and/or cumbersome) that nothing seems to work properly any more, no amount of leadership muscle is going to sort it out in its current configuration. That's just wasted effort. What it needs is to be cut up. Many CEOs and boards will throw up their hands in horror. They are prepared to tinker with the shape of their firm, but wholesale transformation is anathema; they have too much at stake in hanging on to their past. Unfortunately, for very large corporations the first step of the cure has to be radical. The firm must be structured into rational, manageable lines of business.

The task of leadership is to understand this and do something about it at the critical time, rather than persevering with the current (unsatisfactory) structure. We touch here on major change yet again. It's hard to get away from it. Without wishing to stray prematurely into the role of leadership in corporate transformation, reserved for a later chapter, I still want to deal with that element of leadership that must tackle the problem of creating rational chunks of human activity to receive and process information, make decisions and produce a product or a service. Derek Wanless of NatWest calls this 'producing structures with clear objectives in which people operate at their best.'

This might be at the level of the top team configuration, strategic business unit or lines of business, or underneath this in customer service teams. However, it is too often the case that senior management accept the organization structure as largely fixed, either because they are terror-struck by the daunting implications of reorganization, bereft of structural answers or because their own analysis is over-focused on (seduced by) the *effort* observed in various organizational units rather than performance or results. Or maybe it is because leaders have forgotten that it is fundamental to their role to analyse how best to organize the human and machine activity that constitutes 'work' in their enterprises. Call it 'engineering the company' or call it plain old 'organizing', the purpose should be the same. Says John Clark:

> In today's markets the customer focus drive is now essential, therefore your people have to be segmented to provide service appropriate to different customer segments. You cannot have the old control structure sitting on top of these service delivery teams. It won't work. Better to have your management information system providing the basics of control through the fundamental building blocks of the service delivery teams.

Achieving a rational structure which effectively channels organizational energy depends, first and foremost, on the shape of the top team, where, according to Nelson Robertson at General Accident, size does matter. 'Our old management committee was too big', he says. 'For us I believe that anything more than about ten is too big. The dynamics stop it working effectively … . There *is* a drain on my time when the team is too large, but that's not the crucial thing. There's a balance to be struck between a large number of reports, who provide a host of data but spread me and others too thinly, and a very small number, which therefore frees up my time but provides too little information for me to know what the total picture is in the business.'

Not getting the total picture is the point at which the CEO and the top team start to malfunction. The absolute number of members is irrelevant, as Robertson intimates. The nature of the top management tasks (dictated by the nature of the business *as it changes*), the assignment of clear responsibility and accountability, and the absolute prerequisite that the leaders of the business are not insulated from the day-to-day reality of the business and its environment – these are the relevant factors in structuring the top team. Integral as well is the process of decision-making, of converting data into relevant action. 'The team cannot be too large,' insists Peter Ellwood of TSB, 'because this inhibits the quick decisions needed to resolve issues.'

But further down the structure, complex organizations need complex checks and balances to ensure that the right decisions are taken. It seems axiomatic. And the evidence around us shows that managers spend extraordinary amounts of time engaged in meetings of one kind or another, or in sifting data, analysing, examining options, coming to decisions ... Or do they? In the real world meetings drag on without conclusion, data is passed up and down without decisions and without resulting action.

'I want to prevent people,' asserts Hans Boom, 'from just spending time in meetings doing nothing. I want people making decisions, not talking about it. That's why I want as simple a structure for formal decision-making as possible. The first thing I want to know when I set up the structure is, who takes the decisions? Then, who is responsible for what? Finally, what are the discretionary limits for individuals? Taken together the decision-making process is very simple, like this:

'It needn't be any more complex. Data gets turned into information on which the individual makes a decision.'

Would that it were so simple! But the intention is absolutely valid. Boom is urging a straightforward commitment to, first, making decisions (instead of thinking or talking about it) and, second, making decisions as close to the point of receiving data as possible, which is nearest the customer, whether external or internal. If this means changing or rearranging responsibilities, then so be it. Over-reliance on existing hierarchies of authority is part of the traditional command structures that are unsuited to – not to say downright foolish in – the realities of the twenty-first Century.

Generally, throughout the business world there has been a realization that the old structures suppress initiative and destroy the willingness of employees to solve problems in the front line where it counts. Many organizations are doing something about this. Many have gone too far or have done the wrong things. There is no point in delayering or re-engineering a business if these efforts ultimately cost the organization more or satisfy customers less or restrict firms to an emaciated 'core' business whose growth and prospects are fading. There is every point, however, in doing *anything* – unpredictable, unthinkable, risky – if it delivers what customers want and anticipates their needs. It will fail, though, if a leader falls at the first hurdle and cannot rationally structure human activity to generate critical mass. Bill Cockburn neatly summarizes this:

> No matter how bold you are or how inspiring, you can't just rely on chance or hope to get it right. A leader must have the support of a strong managerial and operational infrastructure.

Top Team Leadership or Groupthink?

Every senior management group operating closely as a team will be advantaged (in terms of their effectiveness) by the level of cohesion of the group (how well the members get along, trust each other, etc.). At the same time, however, individual members will at times hold views or opinions divergent from the group view. This may be the result of different personalities seeing things in different ways or members possessing different sources of information. We have all observed this in management teams.

But what is less obvious – even hidden – is the underlying tendency for the team to actively absorb diverging opinions, in short to move all members towards uniformity of opinion. In some circumstances this is a good thing; it ensures that the team reaches conclusions and produces action. In other circumstances the result can be disastrous.

A weighty body of psychological research demonstrates the dangers. Take your average top management team or executive committee. At some point one or two individuals will hold views that are at odds with the group's, for instance in regard to the advisability of a particular strategy. These individuals may also find it impossible to move the group towards their own viewpoint yet still remain less than convinced by the group's arguments and explanations. Where the top team is cohesive (for example, the individual members have co-operated well in the past), it will also be difficult for the individuals to reject the team as whole. The effect on the individual is a state of tension called 'cognitive dissonance' – being pulled in different psychological directions – first described in 1957 by psychologist Leon Festinger. The worrying part of this is that the individual's cognitive dissonance is not typically resolved in favour of a debated compromise between all team members. Far from it; the majority of individuals will relieve this state of tension by shifting abruptly to wholesale adoption of the group's view while suppressing their original views and their own misgivings. Where they don't, groups themselves will act to resolve the tension by isolating, even expelling, the deviant members. In time, of course, this practice augments the forces pushing towards uniformity rather than debate and dissent. The phenomenon was later called 'groupthink' by Irving Janis (1972) and is more commonplace in top teams than we might like to believe.

For leaders the important lesson is to ensure that top teams, particularly in their incarnation as committees, are able to make progress and decisions without the everpresent pitfalls of groupthink. Leadership is the key. As a leader you must resolve not to be fully inducted into the in-group pressures that work inevitably towards conformity; the leader is never just a team-member. You should also be alert to the symptoms of groupthink, as Janis described them, in your own team:

- a sense of invulnerability (with unbridled optimism and risk-taking);
- repeated rationalizations by team-members to downplay threats or difficulties;
- a belief in the team's own inherent morality (ignoring morally questionable decisions or actions);
- stereotyping opponents as stupid or weak;
- the exercise of pressure on individuals who question the team's actions;
- self-censorship of deviations from the team's consensus decisions;
- silence taken as consent; and
- the selective exclusion of contrary information.

The Gentle Art of Persuasion ...

'In getting people to do things they don't want to do but you know are necessary,' Nelson Robertson contends, 'there is a balance to be struck between aggression and tact. The basic rule I follow is that you don't want to upset people needlessly. That requires sensitivity; how far can you go with a particular individual?' It is clear that leaders must understand the people who work for them and many of the leaders I interviewed spoke about building consensus, but in an environment best described by Robert van Gelder:

> I have a position of influence but not power. I can't get things done except through persuasion, manœuvring, and consensus-building.

The effectiveness of leaders at any level depends more and more on their ability to influence people. As hierarchies are disassembled and formal authority is weakened by the need to operate cross-process, cross-function and in networks, so individual influence becomes more important. Yukl, Falbe and Youn (1993, p 7) neatly encapsulate the range of influence tactics available to leaders:

- *Rational persuasion*: logical arguments, facts, and figures in support of particular objectives.
- *Inspirational appeals*: focusing on values, ideals, aspirations or the enhancement of others' self-confidence.
- *Consultation*: participation, willingness to adjust a viewpoint or approach in dealing with concerns and suggestions.
- *Ingratiation*: praise, flattery, friendship or help to predispose others to comply.
- *Personal appeals*: calling upon loyalty, friendship.
- *Exchange*: offers of reciprocation or sharing benefits in accomplishing an objective.
- *Coalition tactics*: seeking the aid of others to exercise persuasion or the fact of their support as a reason for others to comply.
- *Pressure*: demands, threats, constant checking or reminders to produce compliance.
- *Legitimating tactics*: claiming authority, right of legitimacy or verifying the consistency of a request or demand in line with organizational policy, rules, practices and traditions.

The point is to use the right tactics in the right circumstances, taking account of both short-term outcomes and longer term implications. There is no advantage in constantly relying on pressure tactics if this eventually breeds a risk-averse culture devoted to self-protection. Nor is it beneficial to prefer only socially acceptable tactics, at least effort and cost, which frequently fail, thus continually forcing leaders into follow-up escalation to tougher and riskier influence attempts. One of the questions leaders have to answer when they are trying to accomplish important objectives is whether they are seeking commitment or simple compliance. Both are legitimate aims, but are pursued with different goals in mind. The former engages the individual in willingness to take responsibility and to add value; the latter shifts responsibility (in everything except perhaps name) straight back to the leader. The same is true even if, as some people might argue, leaders who expect employees to be committed to the leader's own values are really engaged in a form of manipulation aimed at obtaining compliance through commitment. The distinction lies in the willingness of employees to take responsibility and to add value.

Exercising influence with an eye to the best possible outcome can take quite a lot of manœuvring. 'In meetings it's important to give people a say,' says Simon Dyer of the Automobile Association, 'but the real persuasion takes place outside the meeting, particularly with the non-executives. This in turn requires a great deal of effort to identify the possible sticking points early on to avoid delays or misunderstandings.'

After his appointment at Chep, Alex Watson soon determined that tackling one element of strategy would help another. 'I tried to describe to my top 75 managers,' he says, 'what my vision was of where we could take the business, but I did this by getting *them* to produce the plans for achieving it, with specific individuals tasked and identified with parts of the total plan. I also got most of them into cross-European workgroups so that regional barriers and regional thinking were steadily being broken down.' This was not the end of the story though. Some dyed-in-the-wool managers were not to be convinced of the changes Watson was driving, so he used a time-honoured method: 'I threw people into working groups with colleagues that I knew were believers. Basically, the message has been that the march is not going to be held up by the stragglers.'

The art of manœuvring and persuasion is largely underpinned by judgement, surveying the multiple influences on a situation and then looking beyond. 'There are times,' says Nedcor's Junior Potloane, speaking of meetings with some of his White managerial colleagues to discuss the implications of South Africa's Reconstruction and Development Plan on banking strategy, 'when I could have become confrontational, but I reminded myself that I'm not in the business of winning battles rather than the war.' Scottish Power's Ian Preston expresses the case in a similar way: 'I have sometimes pulled back from driving hard because it became clear that there were bigger fish to fry.'

Nevertheless, a leader's role is sometimes to push hard, especially when major change demands action. Preston again: 'If you're in the throes of a major change programme like we are, there's only room sometimes for consultation and not consensus. Consensus is for the stable environment ... but who's stable these days?' Point taken. Preston goes on to say, however, that people will accept consultation rather than consensus when the argument is compellingly made 'on the basis of rational logic'. Peter Ellwood, too, says of his own efforts at TSB, 'We have been getting better at persuading the larger body of people in the bank through a regular communications programme that emphasizes the logic and intellectual arguments behind our objectives.' The same idea is echoed by Alex Trotman as regards Ford's globalization programme:

> I thought we'd have a much longer adjustment process to get the commitment and drive behind making it work than we have.

The reason?

> Because the power of the logic of the concept is evident to a large body of people ... . The communication between these people has been so effective that the ball is rolling.

Communication by the leaders of a firm is often underestimated. I have frequently heard top managers say, 'People know what they're up against. They know what they have to do.' But communication is not simply about passing on information. Since organizations are still, in virtually every case, authority structures (even if the authority is not a direct reflection of the hierarchy, or lack of it), public pronouncements by leaders are a means of sanctioning action, particularly in major change scenarios. In their book *The Critical Path to Corporate Renewal* (1990) Michael Beer, Russell Eisenstat and Bert Spector report this finding from their research:

> A seemingly endless round of speeches, conferences, meetings, and other methods allowed revitalization leaders to articulate the vision and spread the word about the need for change. These forums helped individuals in the organization understand what revitalization was all about and where it was heading. They kept up pressure for continued forward movement ... . They also granted permission for revitalization throughout the organization ... . Time and time again, unit-level managers pointed to the speeches of corporate revitalization leaders as their rationale for promoting revitalization in their own units. Local managers even engaged in innovations that their peers and immediate supervisors were less than enthusiastic about. (pp191–3)

Leadership and Personal Influence: Some Guidelines

- Ingratiation is sometimes useful for influencing subordinates and peers, but it is seldom useful for an immediate influence attempt with the boss.
- Exchange tactics are sometimes useful for influencing subordinates and peers, but they are seldom useful for influencing the boss.
- Ingratiation should be used in an initial influence attempt rather than in a follow-up influence attempt.
- Pressure tactics should be used in a follow-up influence attempt rather than in an initial influence attempt, and only when justified by the importance of the request.
- Legitimating tactics should be used only when there is a clear, verifiable basis for a request that is unknown to the target.
- A strong form of rational persuasion (for example a clear explanation for the reason for the request or proposal, a review of evidence supporting it) should be used rather than a weak form whenever possible.
- Rational persuasion may be used in combination with any of the other tactics, and it usually increases their effectiveness.
- Ingratiation should be used with another compatible tactic, such as rational persuasion or inspirational appeals, rather than alone.
- Pressure should be used with another compatible tactic, such as rational persuasion or legitimating, rather than alone.
- Strong forms of pressure (for example demands or threats) should not be used in combination with a soft tactic that is based on mutual trust and friendship, such as ingratiation, consultation, or personal appeals.

Yukl, Falbe and Youn
Patterns of Influence Behavior for Managers
Group & Organization Management (1993, pp26–7)

... and the Not-so-gentle Art of Putting Sweat on Brows

'When it was clear to everyone in the organization,' says Peter Ellwood of TSB, 'that our backs were against the wall, it was much easier to act in those circumstances.' Leaders know that a crisis is a trigger and a justification for action of a kind that goes beyond the norm. The advantage is temporary, however, and must be seized firmly. In this, Ellwood was assisted because he was an outsider, newly appointed (remember the value of *disconnection*) and, he admits, 'I was therefore able to wield a big axe among people I hadn't known for 20 years.' Similarly, a number of tactics that come under the headings *creating adventure* and *taking the organization by surprise*, as explored in Chapter 5, also get the ball rolling, to use Alex Trotman's expression, but do not sustain action. Critical mass is achieved in other ways.

Ellwood talks about 'creating a sense of urgency, which must come from the top.' His sentiments are closely mirrored by Bill Cockburn's notion of 'restlessness, driven down to other management layers.' Ian Preston makes the point about his own behaviour: 'I am a link in a chain. If I don't clear things quickly – mail, decisions, you name it – a host of other people are affected.' So, this ongoing sense of urgency is not something leaders just talk about now and again. Nor do they promote it as valuable in its own right, but as a hard-nosed rationale for improving individual, business unit and corporate performance. Alex Watson described the early months after his appointment at Chep:

> I found I had to push the business very hard in the direction I wanted it to go. That meant I had to take out a number of the poorer performers at senior levels and I said to several: 'The pace of change is hotting up. I want to see some sweat on brows.'

Keeping sweat on brows, however, is only useful when people are sweating over the right things. 'It's a waste of time,' insists Hans Boom, 'to discuss the things we agree on. Let's discuss the things we don't agree on. I like to polarize; to make clear what we agree on and then debate the things we don't agree on.' The result is sustained pressure to act and act again, in a direction aligned with overall strategy.

Derek Wanless of NatWest talks about the implementation of the balanced business scorecard as a systematic way of sustaining critical mass in all the units of a complex business. At NatWest the balanced scorecard has been a way of shifting managers and staff away from an over-focus on short-term financial measures in the control of business performance among the operating units and towards longer term financial health. For example, traditional financial indicators such as return-on-investment or sales volume cannot help a firm to reinforce the importance of building customer relationships or completing internal projects to time and cost; these metrics never appear in business performance measurement systems. 'We use the scorecard,' Wanless says, 'to provide a stretching leap to push people along continuously. This keeps people up with the pace and direction of change in our markets.'

Dave Bowyer of Megapak is likewise concerned about the need to review strategy so that Megapak's business performance is much less subject to peaks and troughs. 'Given time,' he says, 'I'll be able to build significant teams that will work together, making better decisions, in particular on the strategic front. Our strategic plan can't be just a document that gets pulled out once a year, dusted off, then put back in the drawer again. It's a *live* thing: we want a monthly review of strategy so that everyone is operating to the most up-to-date information.'

Whether critical mass is initiated via the channels of organizational structure or personal persuasion, and sustained through the deliberate creation of a sense of urgency at every level, leadership is nonetheless at the centre of it.

Focusing Critical Mass – The Balanced Scorecard

Today's managers recognize the impact that measures have on performance. But they rarely think of measurement as an essential part of their strategy. For example, executives may introduce new strategies and innovative operating processes intended to achieve breakthrough performance, then continue to use the same short-term financial indicators they have used for decades, measures like return-on-investment, sales growth, and operating income. These managers fail not only to introduce new measures to monitor new goals and processes but also to question whether or not their old measures are relevant to the new initiatives.

The balanced scorecard ... provides executives with a comprehensive framework that translates a company's strategic objectives into a coherent set of performance measures. Much

---

> more than a measurement exercise, the balanced scorecard is a management system that can motivate breakthrough improvements in such critical areas as product, process, customer, and market development.
>
> The scorecard presents managers with four different perspectives from which to choose measures. It complements traditional financial indicators with measures of performance for customers, internal processes, and innovation and improvement activities.
>
> Kaplan and Norton
> 'Putting the Balanced Scorecard to Work'
> *Harvard Business Review* (1993, p134)

Once it's Moving, Let go!

'I'm trying to create an empowered culture,' Simon Dyer says, 'so that everything we do is much more customer-focused; what does the customer want from us, rather than what we want from the customer ... . Empowerment will also shorten the development timescale for new products and services and especially our major IT projects. But that means we have to sort out the "doers" from the "sit-and-think" brigade ...'

Dyer is articulating the bind in which business leaders find themselves when they try to generate critical mass. If the employees 'down there' could only grab the opportunity to start changing the way they work or co-operating with cross-functional colleagues to improve a key process etcetera, etcetera, then this business would be unbeatable. But they don't – usually. Energy and momentum get eaten up in the bowels of the organization, critical mass is never reached and the whole thing grinds on in the same old way.

Part of the problem is second-guessing managers or staff all the way down the layers. I recall one CEO who had structured his highest levels into a small executive committee of five members and a larger management committee, around fifteen. The two had (apparently) different agendas, the former strategic, the latter operational. The CEO chaired both. In the management committee he was therefore able to regularly countermand or undermine the initiatives of his executive reports. This he justified on the grounds that many of these matters were too important for him to ignore or that his executives had got it wrong. This was bad enough for the executives, but it also rapidly engendered a culture throughout the hierarchy of defensiveness, back-covering and uncertainty. In effect, only one person was in control. Only one person could make real decisions – the CEO.

The opposite extreme is equally horrifying. Empowerment has been taken too far in some organizations. The result is a travesty of individualistic effort and initiative unconnected to the business context and strategy. Employees are given the freedom to operate but remain firmly barricaded inside their bunkers with little conception of the impact on other bits of the business of any change they may make. Co-ordination is important in this regard, but leadership more so. Leadership is not unburdened by empowerment. On the contrary, it makes the burden heavier because the risk is greater and the need for absolute clarity and absolute focus in business direction becomes paramount. None the less, the risks are outweighed by the benefits. Hans Boom:

> Many times I've taken out layers of responsibility, the people who check what other people are checking on the people who do the work, so that *real* responsibility lay with the right person – with the person doing the work or closest to the customer. The reaction every time is tension because of the new responsibilities, but people are also highly motivated because they are treated as capable and they've got no one else to blame or thank.

The same is true when it comes to major change. Not infrequently, leaders make the mistake of handing the whole thing over to consultants. 'It gets very dangerous,' one executive told me once, 'when consultants come to be a crutch for management. When this happens, management is abrogating responsibility for decisions. At that point you are no longer a manager.' Guidance, assistance, leading-edge thinking, extra resource – in the postmodern organization all these things must be sought, but abrogation of responsibility to outsiders or to too-high a level of management is a death-knell. Alex Trotman emphasizes the role of responsibility and empowerment in achieving Ford's programme of change:

> If you're thinking about making a major change, don't have a study team or a staff figure out how to make the change ... . Involve the people right from Day One who are going to have to execute the change ... . The knowledge of each other, the knowledge of the issues, the commitment to the resolution of the issues is in the

minds of the people who are actually going to have to make this work now, right from Day One.

The energy behind critical mass then shifts away from leaders and into the teams in the rest of the organization. For example, Bell Atlantic Corporation, a company of 70,000 employees and $13 billion turnover, has driven training right throughout the organization to ensure that employees learn how to approach their job and get things done through the team. This ensures that the primary pressure points for problem-solving and for developing new, more effective ways of working come from the team itself.

Teams of this kind need to be multi-level and either cross-process/cross-functional or tightly networked into other teams. Integrated alliances outside the business between organizations that provide different process capabilities in what McHugh, Merli and Wheeler call 'holonic networks' in their book *Beyond Business Process Reengineering* (1995), operate on the same principle – that acting together is more effective (i.e. competitive) than acting alone. This is particularly important where customer demand is moving towards customized products and services. It is the job of leadership to define the context – that is, tightly networked teams inside the firm, holonic business networks outside – and to ensure that the people in them have the flexibility to maximize the relationships with each other and with their customers.

This really boils down to common sense and trust. Leaders enjoy being able to influence things, to make things happen, to determine the future of the business entity that they control. Isn't it self-evident that employees may feel the same way? Sure, they may not sit on top of the pile and their horizons may be considerably closer, but their aspirations are the same. What they seek is the freedom to act responsibly and the leadership to direct them.

Who Leads the Leaders?

This is an important question. It is not enough to say that leaders lead themselves or that leaders' great ideas are the result of leadership. This is obfuscation. Leadership is not itself a cause of things; it is a description of a complex pattern of behaviour. How is the behaviour produced? How is it maintained? Why are some people great leaders, but not others?

To go even partway towards answering these questions, we must step back from the individual, from the business unit,

---

from the organization, even from the markets in which firms operate. We must look at nations.

In *The Competitive Advantage of Nations* (1990) Michael Porter touches on leadership. He asks the question, 'But where does a leader get the vision and how is it transmitted to cause organizational accomplishment?' He goes on to argue, 'Great leaders are influenced by the environment in which they work. Innovation takes place because the home environment stimulates it. Innovation succeeds because the home environment supports and even forces it. The right environment not only shapes a leader's own perceptions and priorities but provides the catalyst that allows the leader to overcome inertia and produce organizational change.' (p 584)

The responsibility for developing business leaders, therefore, rests not only with the corporate world but with the institutions of a nation itself – with its schools, its educational and industrial policies, and with the willingness of governments to stimulate the competitive challenges that encourage leadership throughout society.

SUMMARY

Generating Critical Mass

1   *Break it down*: create rational chunks of work activity. Get people making decisions not just talking about it.

2   *Manoeuvre, persuade, influence*: use logic and persuasion to gain commitment, pressure to gain compliance. Keep communicating.

3   *Create urgency*: make clear what is agreed, then debate what isn't. Stretch people.

4   *Let go*: empower people, but get them out of their bunkers first. Let the people who have to change, design the change.

8

THE LEADERSHIP OF CORPORATE TRANSFORMATION

Change, Competitive Advantage and Reinvention

It is possible that the trauma of change is now a necessity for most organizations. Chapter 1 was concerned with firms attempting to adjust to shifting market demands, grapple with aggressive new and desperate old competitors, exploit changing technology, and respond to a plethora of emerging customer standards – what was hitherto considered excellence now regarded as the norm, and the goal the satisfaction of unanticipated customer requirements. The prospect of regaining competitive advantage or maintaining it, even exceeding it, is what has persuaded countless organizations to restructure, to rationalize, to cut costs, to collapse management levels and downsize, to re-engineer the business, to revitalize. For some (a minority) these approaches work. For the rest, as Hamel and Prahalad contend, 'they are still in the category of catching up' (1994, p 277). Catching up is surely not good enough. Perhaps not this year, perhaps not next year, but in time disaster looms. Why? What is it about organizations that makes them so difficult to change? What is wrong with the strenuous efforts that promised so much but have produced such pain, such dislocation, such indifferent effect?

One reason, certainly, must be the piecemeal way in which most change efforts are pursued. Attempts at process re-engineering that take no account of strategy formulation (and vice versa) must be at fault. Culture change without changes to business processes is worse than half-baked. Reconfiguration of the business to core competencies without the empowerment of managers to seek new markets again misses the point.

However, this story is not new. Management theorists have been urging organizations to adopt a total systems approach to change for decades. Take a look at these descriptions – and dates:

> ... the process of initiating, creating, and confronting needed changes so as to make it possible for organizations to become or remain viable, to adapt to new conditions, to solve problems, to learn from experiences...
> Lippitt (1969, p 1)

> ... the concern for the vitalizing, energizing, actualizing, activating, and renewing of organizations through technical and human resources ...
> Argyris (1971, p ix)

> ... a long-range effort to improve an organization's problem-solving and renewal processes, particularly through a more effective and collaborative management of organization culture ...
> French and Bell (1978, p 14)

So, if you thought change, renewal and revitalization were novel ideas of the last couple of years – wake up! They've been around since Woodstock and Neil Armstrong. This is not to say that the implementation of new ideas such as business process re-engineering (BPR) is not different in the types of organizational elements tackled. Rather it is to drive home the point that major change that *does not* involve the entire organizational system is not going to deliver real benefit. More than likely it will merely lubricate the old groaning, creaking machine, making it slightly faster, perhaps cheaper to run, but won't change the way it works or what it produces. That's the first point.

The second point is one that a few management theorists are beginning to articulate – perhaps chief among them Hamel and Prahalad in *Competing for the Future* and Goss, Pascale and Athos in their *Harvard Business Review* article of November – December, 1993, 'The reinvention roller coaster: Risking the present for a powerful future'. Both titles emphasize the point. Grasping the future is what counts in the competitive stakes of the twenty-first century. Downsizing, cost-reduction, re-engineering and so forth produce, in essence, lean organizations. Being lean in order to be a nimble organization and then getting – incrementally – leaner to be more nimble is a devilishly tricky strategy. It doesn't do more than enable you to stand still or gain temporary cost advantages. And, obvious to anyone, there is a point of diminishing returns: an emaciated organization is an unhealthy one. When your competitors are passing you by, you have to do more. The more is industry reinvention – that is, not taking your particular industry structure as a given, not accepting your products and services as commodities limited by cost and current customer demand, not relying on accepted industry practice. More is utterly reconceptualizing market opportunities, seeking the 'white space' opportunities, making the organizational and industry 'leaps' that Ford's Alex Trotman advocates (from new technology through to globalization), jumping beyond just 'catching up' to actually shaping a new market and new competitive advantages. Hamel and Prahalad use two phrases which neatly categorize businesses today: 'net advantage creators' and 'net advantage imitators' (p 276). In which category does your company fall?

Goss, Pascale and Athos emphasize similar goals. They exhort companies to invent the future and cite as an example Sir Colin Marshall's declaration 'that British Airways would be the "world's favorite airline" when it ranked among the worst' (p 103). Between the early 1980s and the 1990s, this future was realized. BA now is among the most popular and profitable airlines in the world. Goss *et al* also bring another element of focus; executive reinvention, the capacity to examine and break out of the box within which executives operate. This box is the context of what executives regard as possible and impossible.

Let's take all these themes together – global change, competitive pressures, restructuring and re-engineering, *total* organizational renewal, industry and executive reinvention. What follows from this is a need for an approach which does three things:

- offers business leaders corporate transparency, that is, it helps them to examine and understand the 'mess' with which they are confronted every day: the current position of their organization in respect of its markets, core competencies, competitors and culture;
- gets leaders to break out of the box and redraw their organization's future (creating new markets, new industries); and
- ensures that all the useful tactics of change (BPR, restructuring, culture change) can be integrated, made to coalesce to produce more than simple incremental change.

Tackling this from the other end – where the organization should have got to after achieving real change – we might say that the change must be palpable for all employees, that they behave differently and more effectively than before, that the organization is more effective, that it has significantly shifted its competitive position, that it can innovate and adapt on a continuous basis to new opportunities, challenges or threats and that it is able to adapt through strategic reinvention by changing the rules, both within and outside itself, to create and exploit unanticipated but tangible markets. This feat is the result, in a phrase, of corporate transformation.

The Structure and Sequence of Successful Innovation ... Or Perhaps Not

We are awash with literature on innovation. Management theorists (and many others besides) talk glibly about it. We are told, and tell one another, that it is vital, that businesses will fail without it. And yet we know almost nothing about how it works.

On the one hand we think it is a process. Zaltman, Duncan and Holbek (1973) believe it has discrete steps:

- knowledge about a new possibility exists and leads to awareness by employees that this is an opportunity that could benefit part of the organization;
- employees' attitudes to the potential innovation then form (ranging from enthusiastic approval to outright resistance);
- those in authority then evaluate the potential innovation and decide whether or not to proceed with implementation;
- the innovation is implemented in a trial or series of trials; and
- the innovation becomes implemented in a sustained way.

Innovation, in this view, is linear, progressive, structured, sequential. It appeals to our familiarity with hierarchy, command and control, beginnings and ends.

On the other hand, Schroeder, Van de Ven, Scudder, and Polley (1989) argue that there are six possible (though not exclusive) stages:

- internal or external shocks give rise to innovation;
- the initial idea proliferates ... into several ideas...

↓

↓

- surprises
and unexpected setbacks
always occur;

- old ways of doing things operate side-by-side with the new, gradually meshing together;
- some restructuring of operations and organization occurs; and
- top management are typically involved, particularly earlier on.

In other words, innovation is fluid, overlapping, composed of untidy back-tracking leaps and surprises – perhaps so sudden that it is almost violent.

We are left to ponder. Still, what we can agree on is that the over-hasty scramble to 'get some innovation in the business' in no way guarantees positive organizational change and may even add to overhead. As Nigel King contends, '... an innovation must at least challenge the status quo; it may, however, fail to actually effect change. Innovation is thus not synonymous with *successful* change.' (1992, pp 90–91)

But many firms do introduce innovations time and again. So is there a prescription for gaining at least partial success? Here are a few thoughts:

- The context of continual upgrading and broader thinking about products, services, and ways of operating should be asserted by business leaders and demanded as normal and expected.
- The philosophy and practice of experimentation should be sanctioned by business leaders.
- Business leaders themselves must be seen to act on innovative ideas (for example, committing resource to piloting new ways of operating).
- The firm must interact with customers at a higher and higher level to understand what they need and want.
- Employees must be allowed to operate in project teams that cross functional, departmental and regional boundaries and the teams should have the authority and power to try out new ways of operating.

> • Where outside consultants are used they should be incorporated as part of the project team.
> • Appraisal and reward systems should be linked to successful experimentation.

'It's BPR, Jim, but not as We Know it ...'

If, like me, you get rather confused by the bewildering array of change and process improvement methods paraded at conferences and seminars, in books and the media, here in summary is a list of some of the more important approaches:

- *Business restructuring*: major structural adjustments to existing parts of the business without, however, tackling cross-business processes (for example cutting duplicated functions, merging departments, contracting out, divesting subsidiaries), often with the aim of cutting cost or propping up revenue.

- *Process simplification and redesign*: improvement aimed at support processes (for example, computer and telecommunications networks, or accounting services) usually by means of outsourcing, subcontracting and facilities management, as well as core business processes (such as new product development or supply chains) using simultaneous engineering or Just-In-Time methodologies, again with a cost-reduction objective but also faster time-to-market.

- *Business process re-engineering (BPR)*: more typically in the mid 1990s focused on an organization's entire business system, covering multiple processes to ensure widespread and radical improvement by converting the vertical functional stovepipes of the old organizational structure into faster, more efficient, higher quality horizontal processes that satisfy particular customer needs such as cost or delivery reliability.

- *BPR (the holonic enterprise)*: recognizing that core business processes extend beyond the boundaries of the single organization, McHugh *et al* (1995) describe the creation of a virtual company from a network alliance of businesses whose combined 'best practice' or 'world class' core competencies are together more powerful and more flexible than they would be alone; re-engineering the cross-company core business processes has the goal of serving customers in entirely new ways. A 'virtual' company, therefore, is a configuration of the best core process capabilities (such as new product development, high-speed batch printing or storage) integrated from a number of firms working together.

This list doesn't include change management (the effective facilitation of change initiatives) because it should underpin all of the above approaches, and is especially important to corporate transformation. Nor does it mention corporate renewal or revitalization (concerned chiefly with behavioural adaptation to ongoing change). Let us put these aside for the moment. Instead, let's try to answer the question of the relevance of the above list of process improvement approaches for business leaders faced with the need to change. We should be concerned with only two parameters; the scope of change and the scale of improvement/impact on the market. Figure 8.1 provides a visual marker of where I believe the various approaches sit against these parameters.

Business restructuring, for example, may attempt to change some processes but not cross-business and the impact, at best, will be only a slight or temporary improvement, usually through no more than cost – nothing to sneeze at, I concede, but unlikely to offer businesses sustained competitive advantage. Process simplification goes one better and may achieve 'best practice' status in some key support or business processes – that is, equivalent to the best benchmarked companies. This is good, but you're still not ahead of the game. Whole company BPR may, with sufficient effort and the right strategy, get your firm in line for serious process innovation, placing you in the forefront with other global businesses and perhaps even creating a 'breakpoint' – a previously unattained level of process innovation that takes the market by surprise (for example offering substantially improved quality, reliability or delivery time, such as City Bank's introduction of a 15 minute mortgage approval process) and therefore delivers substantial longer term benefit to the business. The holonic enterprise goes a step further, setting up a virtual company to rapidly deliver customized products and services on demand, constantly reconfiguring to make use of the best core business processes for new market conditions or for entering completely new markets.

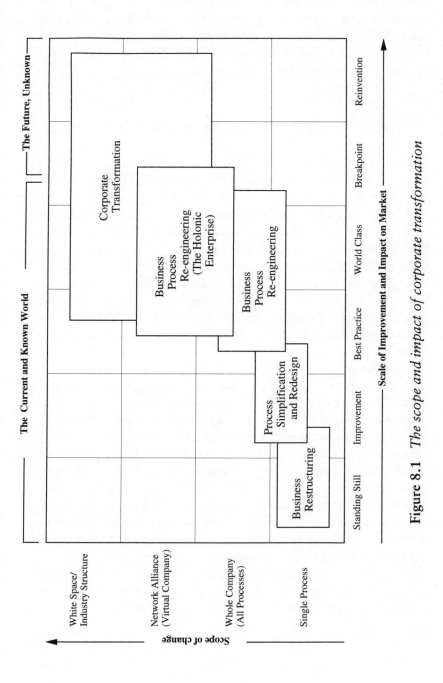

Figure 8.1 *The scope and impact of corporate transformation*

Corporate transformation, as Figure 8.1 shows, extends even further. It is an attempt to get to grips with the future, to go beyond breakpoint advantages in order actively to open up new opportunities, to reinvent markets. Its tactics are, at core, BPR, revitalization, change management, the creation of virtual companies and strategic reinvention.

The Right Leader for the Right Lifecycle?

It used to be said (and indeed still is) that an organization needs different types of leaders at different stages in its lifecycle. We all recognize that the entrepreneurs who start up new ventures and make them successful are often not the best leaders to maintain their rapid success – Apple Computer founder Steve Jobs is the classic example. When Apple got truly big, reaching maturity, his quirky leadership became inappropriate to the needs for stability of a huge business. At a different stage in the organizational lifecycle, IBM's John Akers was unable (despite strenuous efforts) to do anything about the giant's decline. It has required the services of another leader, Lou Gerstner, to make a difference there.

The notion of the organizational lifecycle – illustrated in Adizes' 1988 book *Corporate Lifecycles* – is a useful one because it enables us to step back from the day-to-day task of running a business to see it with the perspective of decades rather than months, in just about the same way that the examination of a person's total life-span tells us something about the pattern of development of normal people at different ages: their needs, their adjustment problems, when they are most productive, what their limits are, what social and psychological experiences and interventions are helpful. Attention to organizational lifecycle tells us important things about organizations and their relationship to their environments. This analogy, as with any, carries a health warning, but it can teach us a bit about the nature of leadership under varying organizational and market conditions. So for our purposes here let's assume two models of the lifecycle:

People	*Organizations*
birth	emergence
infancy	
childhood	
adolescence	growth
puberty	
adulthood	maturity
middle age	
old age	decline
death	decay

Most of the big businesses that management theorists like to write about can be plotted somewhere on the right-hand lifecycle but doubtless most business leaders, of whatever size firm, would be able to say where their organization sits – though not necessarily to admit to terminal decline or decay. Next we need to think about some of the organizational adjustments that firms typically experience (akin to physiological and psychological changes in people as they age). The lifecycle then looks like this:

Lifecycle Stages	*Organizational Adjustments*
emergence	entrepreneurial vision
	innovation/experimentation
	fluid (non)structure
	differentiation
growth	planning
	processes
	structure
	hierarchy
maturity	command and control
	corporate oversight
	technical specialists
	formulaic strategy
	technical improvement
	bureaucracy
decline	rigidity
	technical failure
	risk aversion
decay	retreat from competition
	cultural failure

That's one half of the story. The other is the type of leader. A growing band of writers – for example, Bennis and Nanus

(1985), Tichy and Ulrich (1984) and Avolio, Waldman and Yammarino (1991) – have flirted with the idea that, when it comes down to it, there are only two fundamental types of leader; the *transactional* and the *transformational* leader.

Avolio *et al* enlarge on the distinction:

> Transactional leaders define and communicate the work that must be done by followers, how it will be done, and the rewards followers will receive for successfully completing the stated objectives … .To the extent that transactional leadership can provide greater goal clarity and acceptance of responsibility from followers, the more effective such leadership is over time … .Transactional leadership does not adequately explain why some followers are willing to sacrifice their own self-interests for the good of the leader, their colleagues, or the organization. It also does not adequately explain how some leaders are able to shape the values and heighten the commitment level of followers without any new promise of rewards. (p10)

Translation: transactional leaders engage in an exchange process with followers; 'If you do this, I'll give you that'. The exchange can be explicit (pay for performance) or implicit (cultural messages like 'Let's all do just enough and no one will rock the boat').

Transformational leadership, by contrast, gets people to do far more than they themselves expect they can do. It is commonly described as charismatic or inspirational.

Now, going back to the idea of different types of leaders for different lifecycle stages we can overlay one on top of the other to produce the curve in Figure 8.2. Simply stated, the types of leaders we see in businesses during start-up and early growth tend to be transformational (Steve Jobs at Apple). By contrast, transactional leaders hold the reins when firms are mature, stable and at the peak of their growth (measured across the lifecycle, not against the financial markets' volatile quarter-to-quarter expectations of attractive returns). But transformational leaders also appear when businesses are in trouble and in decline (Lee Iacocca at Chrysler) and, if successful, such leaders shift the entire organization into a new lifecycle.

Here, of course, the analogy with the human lifecycle breaks down. We can't be reborn, organizations can. Chrysler and Ford are good examples. But where the matter gets really interesting is not in the simplistic assertion that organizations should have transactional leaders when stable and mature, and transformational leaders during emergence and growth or as saviours of the terminally ill, but in asking two essential questions:

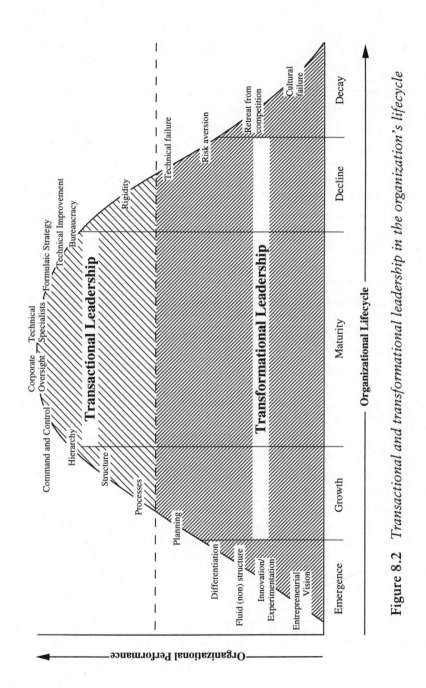

Figure 8.2 *Transactional and transformational leadership in the organization's lifecycle*

- Do organizations of the twenty-first century need to have both transactional and transformational leadership *at the same time*?
- Can the two really be metamorphosed into a single 'Renaissance' leader?

In answer to the first question, the view that leadership behaviour described by the term 'transactional' is sufficient in today's business world is, without putting too fine a point on it, wrong. Any organization – mature, stable, profitable, dominant and unthreatened – is only one step away from catastrophe. IBM proves this point. For 40 years it was all of these things, now it is not. The extreme pain of, among other things, shedding 140,000 IBMers worldwide may have reduced its cost-base and has recently brought the giant back to profitability, but it is now a crippled giant and its nimble competitors can run much faster. Apple Computer was until the early 1990s also light years ahead of its competitors. Now it is struggling. Aggressive discounter Wal-Mart's ousting from pole position of omnipresent US retailer Sears Roebuck (once lauded by Peter Drucker as one of America's most successful enterprises) tells the same tale. In conclusion, transformational leadership is both desirable and necessary in businesses today, and will increasingly become more important. Organizations *must* be capable of fast, radical change and those that aspire to be the best must be able to lead change rather than just follow it. A word of caution, however; remember that perennial revolution is mere anarchy. People and organizations need the balance of the transactional, the creation of a state of order and routine suitable to the realization of economies of scale and corporate stability.

This leads us to our second question – can we have Renaissance leaders? Can transactional and transformational behaviour work successfully in a single leader? Yes, without doubt and more so where leaders can understand the necessity and actively produce both by means of the leadership team. The trouble is we have tended to celebrate one type of leader over the other – the heroic and inspirational over the solid and unexciting. We have also, as I mentioned earlier in this book, allowed the conditions to prevail in most organizations (control instead of risk and opportunism) which emphasize 'transactional' behaviour. The revolutionaries, by contrast, have made their name throughout their careers by being few in numbers and *different*, by always doing revolutionary things in big, boring organizations at a time or in business units that called for revolution.

But when organizations must seek solutions, when they must respond, and fast, while the company is still strong, before the fatal blow, when they must be able to throw off their old cultures and histories, as proud as they are of them, when they must cut costs, delayer, revitalize, fight back, when they must transform themselves – what then is the leader's role?

More of the Same ... and Still More ... It Must Work!

There are objectives within reach ... for the retention of which the French General Staff would be forced to throw in every man they have. If they do so the forces of France will be bled to death, since there can be no question of a voluntary withdrawal, whether or not we reach our goal ... . The objectives of which I speak are Belfort and Verdun ... . The preference must be given to Verdun.

General Erich von Falkenhayn (December 1915)

Falkenhayn's decision to introduce attrition into warfare, namely the deliberate sacrifice of large numbers of your own men on the assumption that the enemy will lose even more than you do, was a logical outgrowth of the idea of total war. In such a struggle every resource must be used, including manpower. However, it was also a tacit admission that current tactical and strategical skills were inadequate to deal with the military stalemate.

Geoffrey Regan
The Guinness Book of Military Blunders (1991, p 25)

We might easily imagine a similar title in the coming century, perhaps *The Guinness Book of Business Leaders' Blunders*, to add to several others already prominently displayed on bookshop shelves. It is puzzling how easily business leaders become entrapped by the same logic scores of generals have displayed over the centuries. The strategies and tactics are depressingly familiar. Faced with aggressive competition, CEOs counter by engaging in a war of attrition; they cut prices, they promote and advertise more, they concentrate enormous resource and effort on the battle with their competitors, they plump for the worst of all strategies – the frontal assault on the enemy. New thinking, new ideas, a different perspective, perhaps the pre-emptive launch of a new product, the concentration on niche markets – all are nowhere on the horizon.

Changing the Rules

Bill Cockburn of the Post Office calls it 'kicking the beast'. I've heard other business leaders talk of 'blowing up the organization'. These phrases are boldly spoken, but I suspect that what underlies them is a genuine appreciation of (and a sense of frustration at) the difficulty of making transformation happen. Nevertheless, if there are any guidelines to be had on the role of leadership in corporate transformation, blowing up the corporation must be among them. There are others and I have distilled from various writers' thoughts, from my own experience and from the wisdom of the business leaders who contributed to this book, a few essentials for the leadership of corporate transformation:

- *Create strategic white space*: explore new options by changing the rules by which you and your business have always played. This means first allowing, then enabling a much wider cadre of managers to get involved in strategizing. If you can't climb out of the box yourself, then get others to pull you out, even if you have to hire people who are not hidebound by your firm's straightjacketing preconceptions. This will also mean encouraging entrepreneurial action, some of which will work and – now here's the rub – some of which will fail. You will not rewrite industry rules by retaining strategic power at the top. You cannot know enough at the top and the old strategic planning methods spell paralysis for strategy-making that is aimed at changing competitive position. Entrepreneurship is about doing things and then analysing them, not vice versa. The leader's role is to draw these individual threads together at the corporate level where size can make the difference in both economies of scale and critical mass in the market. What this demands from leaders is the imposition of context in the business to make it believable and the conviction to sanction it and back it up.
- *Blow it up*: if you are truly committed to transformation or circumstances leave you no choice, then don't pussyfoot. Radical change means *radical*. Nothing is sacred. Nothing should be spared. You have to think of the firm as a blank sheet. Given proactive strategy-making as described above and a good understanding of your firm's core competencies, what structure, processes and culture are needed in order to deliver that strategy? To accomplish this will take time and

you will need help, both from consultancies in terms of ideas and resources and from benchmarking the best processes in *any* industry.

- *Make leaps*: the future cannot be grasped by incrementalist strategies. They are always a day late in comparison to your best competitor, and usually much later than emerging non-traditional competitors. Innovation will get you some of the way there, but don't expect that you can set up a procedure for creativity, or that you can control it. You'll be surprised every time. Innovation is risk. It will emerge best through empowerment of the people who have to make the change, who are closest to the problem or closest to the customer. Empowering people means that the leader must publicly sanction their efforts and explicitly support them in a sustained way. Most people in the organization will be defensive, perhaps surprised. Surprise them again. Unpredictability is a virtue.

- *Create corporate transparency*: transformation of your firm will be messy. The plan will not be the journey. It is hard enough under normal circumstances to see clearly down and through the complexities of large businesses or to keep sight of the future. If it is hard for business leaders, it is doubly hard for everyone else. You must be utterly clear about context, where does this business stand, where has it come from, where is it going, where will transformation take it? You must make data and information work for you not against. You must understand everything about your business as it is, and not as it is presented to you. A reality check is not a criticism of yourself or your managers, it is simply a practical means of avoiding personal and corporate navel-gazing. Finally, you must communicate all the time, both inside and outside the organization. Do not rely on chance – its messages are deceptive.

- *Integrate change tactics*: BPR, restructuring, and culture change will work best in a transformation effort when they are integrated and when they align with emerging (ie changing) strategy. CEOs are the sponsor for transformation. It is not something that can be delegated. It cannot be done by consultants. They can help but they cannot lead it. As a result, it is the job of business leaders to mobilize the right change initiatives, sustain them and ensure that they coalesce. The implication of this is that business leaders must acquire knowledge of the thing they are sponsoring. This is most difficult for those leaders raised in organizational cultures that have stressed control over risk, command over empowerment, caution over opportunity, and consistency over the unpredictable. For some the personal change will be too much – corporate transformation is not for them.

● *Aim for change overload*: organizations, it seems, are slow to change. They relapse. They resist. They protest. Or at least the people in them do. Transformation will not happen unless people are overloaded with change initiatives. Less than overload, as the alternative, is just as painful but produces only incremental change. This is not an exhortation to *force* changes upon people. Persuasion, participation and empowerment are imperative, but corporate transformation asks for more.

Corporate Transformation – Sudden or Gradual?

In a recent book, *Darwin on Man*, Gruber has argued that the concept 'gradual = natural; sudden = miraculous' was a feature of Darwin's thinking from the time he was a student, remaining unchanged during his transition from a belief in the biblical account of creation to an acceptance of evolution ... . For Darwin the essential task facing any theory of evolution was to explain the detailed adaptation of organisms to their ways of life. If this adaptation is to be brought about by the natural selection of variants which are in their origin non-adaptive, the process must involve a very large number of steps, many of them small in extent. To produce a detailed adaptation by means of mutations of large effect only – macromutations – would face the same difficulties as would a surgeon obliged to perform an operation using a mechnically controlled scalpel which could only be moved a foot at a time ... [S]ince existing organisms are well adapted, large mutations are necessarily harmful. I am not fully persuaded of this. I agree that adaptation could not be produced by the selection of macromutations only, but I cannot see why occasional macromutations should not have been incorporated by selection.

John Maynard Smith
Evolution Now: A Century After Darwin (1982, p 125)

Is there an analogy here? Does successful organizational adaptation require a very large number of steps – small mutations of structure, processes, technology, and culture? Is the alternative – big change, all at once – harmful? Can firms leap into the future on the back of radical transformation?

The Leadership of Corporate Transformation

As before, perhaps we are asking the wrong question. Perhaps it is better to ask; should an organization do both? Yes. Occasional transformation is crucial, but the one-off breakthrough will always be temporary in gaining competitive advantage. By contrast, perpetual radical transformation is anarchy, absorbs enormous energy and is ultimately destructive. Much preferable is an organizational lifecycle involving small, regular and rapid changes to structure, processes, technology and culture, sufficient to create competitive space and new advantages in an unforgiving market. Corporate transformation then is both sustained upgrading, innovation and organizational change *and* the proactive response of anticipating seismic shocks from the future – trade liberalization, shifting economic power, unexpected threats – to ensure a quantum shift in competitive position and avoid what follows maturity and stability – decline and decay.

9

THE DEVELOPMENT OF BUSINESS LEADERS – PERSONAL AND ORGANIZATIONAL STRATEGIES

Business Leaders or (just) High Performance Managers?

It is often the case that senior executives publicly confirm that the quality of management is the most important determinant of an organization's future success. They commit immense resources to the task of continually upgrading the quality of people. It is not unusual, for example, for large corporations to be spending $100 million a year on staff and management training alone, excluding on-the-job development and the indirect costs of people's time. And yet for all this investment and the use, in the most committed companies, of sophisticated management development tools, I can't escape the impression that most firms are only succeeding in producing, at best, high performance managers and not leaders.

It would be churlish, I agree, to sound a somewhat sneering note about the success of some organizations in producing high performance managers. On the contrary, I applaud it, but I am in despair at the apparent incapacity of firms to develop leaders. There is a peculiar ignorance and *naïveté* among top managers and human resources professionals when it comes to the development of business leaders – this despite the fact that emphasis on management development has gained considerable momentum during the last two decades. Driven by technological change, redundancies, the characteristic cycle of growth and recession, intensified competition and regulatory changes, firms are demanding more efficient utilization of resources. All very sensible.

Indeed, many large organizations have been pretty successful in setting in place a range of management development tactics which help managers directly in learning new skills or being exposed to a broader array of managerial work, and in accumulating data on the assets, strengths, weaknesses and potential of the management population for use in corporate decision-making – notably, succession, resourcing projects, and facilitating acquisitions or divestments. Businesses have also started to move away from unthinking commitment to their own large leafy-glade management training centres where filling the places on standard training courses is frequently (and horrifyingly) the norm. Likewise, training and development have begun to be seen more in qualitative terms (meeting business needs) than in pure quantitative terms (numbers of courses, costs and so forth).

Moreover, we have begun to understand the fundamental difference between management training and management development. The former is a series of initiatives that are short-term in outlook and intended to enhance existing skills or inculcate new skills to improve an individual's current performance. By contrast, management development is longer term in outlook, is tied to the future of the business and is geared towards building broader skills that will be required for future management roles. It is concerned with identifying and creating a new cadre of management talent, a pool from which the organization may draw to ensure competitiveness in its markets.

There is also a growing recognition that informal, unplanned experiences are crucial for management development. In his book *Management Development* (1989) Alan Mumford reminds us:

> An overemphasis on the 'planned and deliberate' has excluded many of the experiences which are particularly real for managers. The exclusion of those preponderant and powerful experiences is not only illogical but leads to a diminished persuasiveness in talking to managers about development. We have therefore reached a position in which the reality of management development is reversed, so that the minority pursuits of carefully planned and deliberate development experiences have become the only ones recognized as management development! (p 21)

Since it's difficult, not to say impossible, to control and direct such experiences – and the very action of controlling might anyway negate them – there has been increasing emphasis on self-development, with managers making the running about how and what they develop. Of course, this philosophy of development necessitates a detailed understanding of those aspects of the manager's own corporate environment that support or constrain self-analysis and self-development (a manager's boss, for a start).

And so, with the addition and acceptance of more informal methods of development, including self-development, the ponderous beast that is management development has taken some giant steps forward. In the best organizations managers are acquiring varied and more complex skills. They have greater control over their development and, thus, greater motivation to develop further. Self-analysis and analysis of personal competencies through sophisticated methods such as assessment centres, involving job simulations and psychometric instruments, have given managers a much clearer data-set about themselves from which to plan ongoing development action. Project-based experiential learning and cross-functional job moves have enabled managers to extend their business knowledge and commercial acumen on a faster timescale than before. In short, we are generally much better at developing managers – using the methods summarized in Figure 9.1 – than at any time in business history.

But to do the same for leaders is much more difficult, although the reasons are not that obscure. First, we know quite a lot about management. We do not know as much about leadership. Second, it is relatively straightforward to improve managerial effectiveness because you are simply adding progressively to the skills set. Not so with leadership. The patterns of behaviour I have described in this book are qualitatively different, *more than*, the skills of management. I compared this, in Chapter 2, to leaping a gulf. I do not think that leadership develops gradually in the way that managerial effectiveness does, building one skill on top of another. The experiences that together mould leadership in people are much more likely to be sudden, psychologically 'violent' and unpredictable. They confront the individual with dilemmas and the need to resolve personal conflicts and fears of power, authority and success. But these experiences are also likely to be interpreted for the individual by others who can make a difference to the individual *at the time* – through advice, support and simple objectivity. In a phrase, leadership development is about the merit of experience.

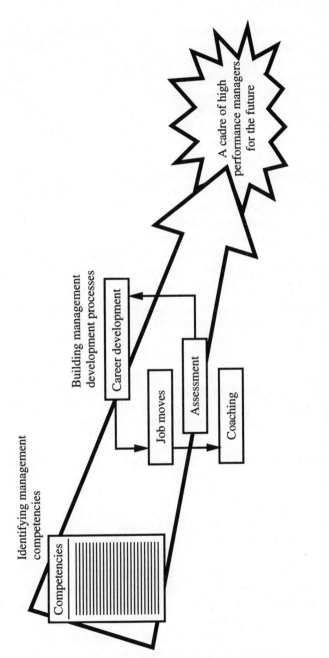

Figure 9.1 *Developing leaders or managers?*

Getting to the Top: How American and British CEOs View the Climb

If you ask business leaders about the major developmental influences in their own career, you get an entirely different picture than the one that has been carefully constructed in their business. While human resource professionals are racing around building training programmes or sending the high potential managers to business schools, even big-ticket 'leadership' programmes at Harvard or INSEAD, their CEOs are suggesting that these activities had little to do with getting *them* to the top slot. In all the time I have spent with senior executives, one theme has repeatedly struck me; how few of them could identify formal training as an important vehicle for their development. They are much more likely to point to significant early responsibility, getting a larger managerial role sooner than expected, working for people who stretched them or having informal mentors who gave sound advice or made opportunities available. Ian Preston of Scottish Power speaks, I think, for many business leaders:

> I was asked to take on challenging roles which I did not refuse. I wasn't frightened by them. I wanted to get away from working *for* others, get away from the constraints that that imposes, have the autonomy to *do* things differently.

Research in Britain and the US confirms this (Margerison, 1980; Margerison and Kakabadse, 1984). The factors that CEOs believed were the major influences in progressing their climb to the top are listed in the table below.

Rank order	Statements	Score (out of 100)
1	Ability to work with a wide variety of people	78.4
2	Early overall responsibility for important tasks	74.8
3	A need to achieve results	74.8
4	Leadership experience early in career	73.6
5	Wide experience in many functions before age 35	67.6
6	An ability to do deals and negotiate	66.4
7	Willingness to take risks	62.8
8	Having more ideas than other colleagues	61.6
9	Being stretched by immediate bosses	60.4
10	Ability to change managerial style to suit occasion	58.8
11	A desire to seek new opportunities	56.8

12	Becoming visible to top management before age 30	56.0
13	Family support	55.2
14	Having a sound technical training	54.8
15	Having a manager early in career who acted as a model	52.0
16	Overseas managerial/work experience	41.2
17	Experience of leadership in the armed forces	40.4
18	Having special 'off-the-job' management training	32.8

The Merit of Experience

Given my earlier comments about the qualitative difference between management and leadership and the implication that leadership must be developed via the merit of experience, you might think that I was admitting defeat, that whatever you try to do (either as an individual or an organization) is hit and miss, more likely to fail than succeed in developing leadership. I am not saying that. Nor am I exhorting a casual, unplanned approach to leadership development, nor a passive acceptance that 'cream rises to the top'. But if we truly are to develop leaders, we must recognize these differences and difficulties.

Alex Watson of Chep in Europe relates a story that typifies the process of becoming a leader. In 1980, while still at Metal Box, he stepped into a new job, a much bigger general management role. That was the Monday. On Tuesday, the workforce of his largest supplier, British Steel, went out on strike (and stayed out for three months). He says:

> It was one of the biggest events of my career. We were virtually 100 per cent dependent on steel *and* on British Steel. Remember, this is Day Two of the new job. I had to get out to speak to a string of my customers, all of whom could smell blood and who were demanding solutions. No one could have *taught* me how to deal with a situation like that. I had to live through it. I learned I had to have contingency plans, take nothing for granted, I had to work with customers all the time, learn from *their* experience, share things with them, and build up trust.

The challenges, difficulties, stresses, successes and even (especially?) the failures of a managerial career are episodes that, taken together, forge the experience that equips managers to leap the

149

gulf to become leaders. John McCoy of Banc One puts it simply and bluntly:

> You learn more by failure itself, than by my telling you you've failed or how you might fail …

To leverage off the merit of experience, we must bring together a mix of the formal and the informal, the personal and the organizational. The five elements listed below sum up the approach:

- the leadership domain;
- analogue and work-based assessment;
- cross-business moves;
- self-development; and
- external mentoring.

Soft Competencies, Hard Outputs and the Leadership Domain

For some time behavioural competencies have been infiltrating every corner of every large organization in the world. The concept has left its mark. There are even university degrees up for grabs in the management of competence. The force behind the competence movement has been a need clearly to specify the precise skills, abilities, knowledge and personal characteristics required for particular jobs – from simple shopfloor roles up through every layer of management. The idea works quite well. It gives employees a solid picture of what outputs are expected in a particular job and what skills, abilities and so on will help to produce the defined outputs. So it facilitates performance effectiveness and the acquisition of new skills as jobs change or customers demand new services and higher standards.

Unfortunately the business world I have described throughout this book is moving faster than that. Competencies cannot be updated sufficiently quickly to *tell* employees what knowledge is needed to perform a rapidly evolving job in a rapidly changing organization. Nor do they enable staff and managers to leap ahead, to innovate, to step outside the box. This problem is magnified countless times in leadership roles. The five chapters in the middle of this book have been an attempt to dissect leadership and define, not competencies, but the broad patterns of behaviour that enable leadership to work, to produce complex outputs that *significantly* enhance the competitive position of a business on a day-to-day basis. It is impossible to know what those outputs will be. Certainly no book could be written on them. They change from moment to moment. Competition among organizations never achieves equilibrium. It is *dynamic*. If the business world of the twenty-first century is a storm-lashed ocean, then imposing context, risk making and risk taking, unpredictability, conviction and generating critical mass are the captain's means of keeping the organizational ship afloat, of changing tack and taming wind and ocean to the great vessel's advantage.

If you aspire to leadership (or more complex levels of leadership), ask yourself this question: to what extent have the five elements of leadership been encouraged in your career? Not often, I'll bet. If you are the CEO, ask yourself whether your organization facilitates the development of talented individuals in the leadership domain. Read the list below and reflect:

● Strategy-making, unravelling and making sense of organizational and market complexity are tasks kept close to the top of firms so that middle managers and young executives never have the opportunity to explore and impose context in their bit of the business.

● This is also, depressingly, true of risk. Managers develop an understanding of risk, opportunity and risk-taking in spite of the organization, not usually because of it. Risk is monitored, managed and avoided. Opportunity is guarded at the top echelons.

● Unpredictability is undesirable; organizational and cultural conformity oppresses it and does the same to innovation and white space thinking. Stability, consistency and equilibrium are valued over experimentation.

● Have you tested your convictions? Are you expected to have any? How has your boss reacted? With encouragement? Dismissively? Would your organization take a risk on something you propose because of your utter conviction?

● Are you empowered to try things, to make things happen? Do you empower others? Do you trust them?

Organizations are not good at developing these skills in managers. Individuals shy away and seek the safe option. Why be different? But remember, to be different is to be a leader.

Diving Under the Microscope: Analogue and Work-based Assessment

Much attention in businesses has been focused on individual performance assessment and on assessment for potential. However, comparatively little work is being done to assess managers against the domain of leadership. Performance appraisal as it is generally used is inadequate to the task – primarily because it is concerned with indicators of current performance. Assessment centres are helpful, if they are really an 'analogue' or slice of the more senior leadership role. They afford managers an excellent opportunity to have a go at the target job, if only for a day or so, and the resulting data-set can be very useful to the individual in self-development and career planning. In turn, the organization gains an objective view of the manager's future potential, strengths and development needs.

But assessment centres are not a slice of leadership reality in the same way they can be for managerial life. At best, they approximate. For example, it is difficult, to say the least, to assess risk-taking. The other elements of leadership are similarly problematical. They are not competencies (directly linked to defined areas of job output) and therefore it is hard to design job simulations that bring them out. But don't give assessment centres the heave-ho just yet; they assess the fundamentals of management behaviour better than any other method. An assessment centre, incorporating appropriate psychometric instruments as well as job simulations designed to reflect managerial work and culture in your organization accurately, can prove very valuable in assessing a whole range of managerial competencies. A typical profile of competencies for a senior general manager might be the following:

Business orientation
- strategic thinking
- awareness of the business
- commercial acumen
- customer focus

Judgement/decision-making
- information gathering
- analytical thinking
- judgement
- decisiveness

Organizing and managing
- planning
- managing people
- organizing work
- developing others

Personal style
- interpersonal skills
- impact and influence
- initiative
- resilience

Most firms train up their own senior managers to act as observers or assessors on assessment centres. This has the value of reinforcing the role of line managers in developing people. However, there is also a lot to be said for using external assessors for senior management assessment and development, as long as the external assessors are seasoned business people themselves and are therefore able to comment on managers' development needs in strategic thinking, commercial appreciation and general business knowledge. Unfortunately, many providers of assessment services focus exclusively on the softer competencies, and the same can be said of too many in-house management development programmes at the largest organizations.

Assessing leadership potential is a somewhat different matter. I offer below a few suggestions:

- Understand, first of all, that the leadership domain is very different from managerial competencies. Know what it is you're trying to assess – both the competencies (the bedrock of management) and leadership.
- Communicate what you mean by leadership to the whole organization. If it terrifies you to explain to your firm that risk and unpredictability are valued, you need to first change yourself and then your firm. Leadership cannot thrive in an organization that mouths the words but extinguishes the first spark of leadership that emerges.
- Task potential leaders with short projects (particularly cross-business projects) that demand action across boundaries and the need to manage people and complex issues. Such projects must be challenging, for example when they are in addition to a manager's normal role and will make a significant difference to business performance.
- Solicit feedback from a wide range of people on the potential leader's performance on projects, but do this systematically. It is crucial to find out whether a manager is really exposed to risk or has genuine accountability for a decision.
- Faced with senior level succession (to business unit head, onto the Board or into the CEO slot), load the contenders with larger roles and additional responsibilities and see how they perform. Do not pretend that succession at that level can be accomplished in a polite, friendly atmosphere. Leadership positions are valuable. People fight for them. Why ignore the obvious? Turn it to advantage and create positive competi-

tion. The contender who fails to get the top role may leave, but that is far preferable than sweeping ill-feeling and aggression under the carpet.

What cannot praise effect in mighty minds
When flattery soothes and when ambition blinds!

John Dryden
Absalom and Achitophel

From Stove-pipes to Cross-business Spirals and Beyond

Organizations built on functional lines have tended to produce specialists. This was especially the case up until the late 1970s and 1980s. Downsizing over the last decade has forced organizations to make better use of managers, consequently obliging individuals to take on wider roles or move to functions away from their traditional career route. All things being equal, senior management effectiveness is driven directly by breadth of business acumen. By building up wide experience of all functions and markets and of several competitive scenarios – restructuring, rapid growth, acquisition, divestment, start-up – commercial experience and business thinking are materially enhanced. This cannot be achieved by functional stove-piping – cutting managers off from wider business realities during the course of their careers.

In Japan, in a national culture that values and promotes service longevity, it has long been the practice to expose managers to as many new organizational and business experiences as possible and also to ensure that they have solid grounding in every function – production, marketing, finance, personnel, sales, and research and development. Thus, young managers are moved from one job to another every two or three years and may be transferred to other offices and plants. The long-term objective is to develop managers who will be more valuable to the company as they rise up the escalator of the Japanese seniority system known as *nenko joretsu*. The image I think that describes this best is an upward development spiral across all functional areas of the business.

Creating exactly the same system in western organizations is not an option. Service longevity in the West is becoming less common rather than more. Still, the lesson is important. Management development must start early in an individual's career. I have frequently seen high casualties result from initiatives aimed at fast-track development of middle and senior managers when they have not had the opportunity, much earlier in their careers, to broaden their skills sufficiently to cope with more senior appointments. The development has come too late.

All of this applies equally to the development of potential leaders as it does to high-performance managers. There is no substitute for early experience in running as many parts of a business as possible. Where structure makes this difficult, a series of cross-business projects is the next best thing. Beyond this, however, there is enormous value to be had from two types of business experience:

- jobs in *other* firms; and
- the opportunity to operate at board level four or five years before you're ready.

Am I serious? Yes. Can it be done? Yes. Firstly, having a number of jobs during your career in different organizations is becoming a must. Gaining an outside point of view is a catalyst for problem-solving. You learn to operate with different business models. You have a basis for challenging organizational and cultural norms. You see the firm with *perspective* – disconnection.

Secondly, board experience can be gained through independent or non-executive directorships in subsidiaries or in separate firms outside your industry or market. This is already happening in several organizations as a deliberate effort to equip senior managers, still four to eight years away from board-level positions, with the experience to operate in the complex, high-pressure environment of top management. What the host organizations gain from this arrangement is access to specific industry, commercial or technical knowledge from the individual non-exec. Non-execs themselves might commit two days a month to this additional role and must not only get to grips with the details of strategy and business operations at board meetings, but exercise persuasion and influence among other non-execs and, especially, with the executive team. Without independent directorships, this kind of experience – an invaluable leap into the future – is otherwise denied to younger, fast-track managers.

Remember, too, that responsibility for actioning this is not just a job for the human resources or training function; it rests ultimately with the top team. 'Succession exercises me considerably,' declares John Clark of BET. 'I am always looking to groom people behind me. In the 1990s, to be a legitimate CEO candidate you will need multiple experience in different businesses and in the lifecycle of organizations. I will move people at any time to any business. Most don't like the change, but they recognize the way to develop and advance.'

The difference between managers and leaders in this regard will be in their perception of the size of the challenge. Partly this is a personal thing. Bill Cockburn relates this anecdote:

> When I joined the Post Office there was a culture of seniority, not merit. You had to put yourself out to seek advancement. I was somewhat less than satisfied when my first boss, who thought he was being encouraging, told me: 'If you work hard and do the right things you can be in my position in 20 years.' As it happened, 20 years later, almost exactly, I was on the Board!

The point here is that leaders seek and make their own opportunities. They want more than the average challenge. To develop leaders (and, in the twenty-first century, to avoid losing them to a competitor), organizations must get smart about testing managers' determination to succeed. My suggestions for accomplishing this are:

- Abolish functional stove-pipes. (Process re-engineering is doing away with them anyway.) Move managers around from the moment they start their career. It will quickly be apparent who wants and can do more and who prefers to be a specialist. Nothing wrong with being a specialist, but it makes it much harder to lead a business unit or an integrated corporation.
- Keep an eye on track-record. Leaders will grab their chances and prove their worth, on projects and in new jobs.
- Arrange, where possible, non-exec or independent directorships for your brightest and best. This is both an excellent test of their mettle and a chance for them to 'speed-learn' about leadership in top management.
- Take risks. Promote high-potential managers sooner rather than later.
- Forgive the odd mistake. We all make them. Managers who have never put a foot wrong are hiding behind someone else's leadership.

They say best men are moulded out of faults;
And, for the most, become much more the better
For being a little bad.

William Shakespeare
(Mariana in *Measure for Measure*)

Fear of Failure, Fear of Success: Self-development

In a rapidly changing business world, providing managers with the freedom and responsibility to enable them to generate their own individual development strategies is an important way of acquiring new skills or overcoming shortcomings. It avoids the considerable time frequently wasted in off-the-shelf courses geared to the 'average' group of managers. It can also establish more clearly the link between personal and business needs – how development can benefit individuals in their current and future roles as well as fulfiling organizational requirements (for example, leading process re-engineering projects, launching a new service or product, contributing to strategy formulation). Self-development also transfers the learning emphasis away from 'thinking about things' to action, away from the classroom to the business imperatives of the managerial and leadership role.

More than this, though, self-development is a process for individuals to expand the data-set about themselves continually – about their strengths, their weaknesses, their convictions and their careers. Leaders are willing to learn. They will acknowledge errors early and do something about it. They will take action. 'I wasn't a very good accountant,' says the Automobile Association's Simon Dyer about the start to his working career, 'so I quit Coopers & Lybrand!'

Koos Radebe, at the SABC, spent his early working years as an announcer and broadcaster and, thrown in the deep-end of management, realized that he needed to broaden his business and general management skills fast. He took a couple of degrees and then a Masters degree in management through the business school of the University of the Witwatersrand in Johannesburg. 'In my early days [of management] I made mistakes,' he acknowledges,

157

'but I learned valuable lessons and I also analysed the shortcomings of other radio stations so that when I started at Radio Metro in 1986 I was able to make a success of it.'

Self-development is about positioning yourself as well. Derek Wanless at NatWest Group:

> I had a succession of great jobs, but I made sure I got offered particular jobs because I thought they were the right ones to get me into general management. It took some manœuvring, on occasion deliberately avoiding the popular, glamorous jobs – in International for example – because I judged it was more important to be in Head Office at that time.

The types of job you get and the psychological growth forced upon you by some of the toughest management challenges are a large part of leadership development. They amount to what I mean by the 'merit of experience'. Some of these challenges – to do with handling apparently insurmountable tasks, or getting to grips with a totally new business in all its technical complexity, or rescuing some venture from the brink of disaster – are well documented but, in my experience, are not necessarily the true challenges of leadership development. We must look deeper to discover those.

Perhaps most important of all is the simple challenge of stepping into a significant leadership position. All you have to do is take on the job, but the cardinal error committed by many executives is believing that what has made them successful in a succession of senior roles is what is going to make them successful in the new one. More senior leadership roles get bigger and more complex. Leaders *must* play themselves in. They must develop themselves.

In 1963 Abraham Zaleznik tackled, in a paper for the *Harvard Business Review*, what he called "The human dilemmas of leadership'. He was concerned that there had been little intelligent analysis of the very real dilemmas confronting leaders in the exercise of power and authority. *HBR* reprinted the paper in 1989 in a collection entitled *People: Managing Your Most Important Asset*. Zaleznik's concerns are as relevant now as they were in 1963. One of his main observations is that managers on the way to becoming leaders need to take the elementary step of assuming responsibility for their own development. In doing so they start to face and deal with the conflicts and dilemmas of attaining leadership positions.

The first dilemma is the problem executives confront almost overnight after promotion. Suddenly, people who were peers are more cautious, distant and constrained. Colleagues at the new level abruptly become competitors. And so the dilemma is between the exercise of authority and the need to be liked. Those who play down their authority and concentrate on being liked end up being immobilized, especially when tough action is called for. Subordinates may even regard the bosses who do this with contempt; they are ineffective and they are less than subordinates expect them to be. Ian Preston of Scottish Power says flatly:

> You have to be able to be aloof. You can't have friends in the management team. You can have friendly relationships, but not friends – if you're tempted, you need to remind yourself that one day you may have to fire them ...

A similar dilemma is manifest in the sense of loneliness that comes with leadership positions. Individuals may shy away from making hard decisions (which at senior level are often going to be controversial) because of the fear of aggression and retaliation from other powerful figures both in the firm and outside it. Leaders cannot please everyone, nor should they attempt to do so. They may often provoke dismay, anger and vigorous challenge. Learning to have an opinion and stick to it is the lesson of conviction. We should never pretend it does not require great courage or, in the obverse, even greater courage to back down in the face of persuasive logic. Ultimately, for leaders whose ambition combined with their conviction has left them well and truly out of touch, believing themselves omnipotent, the reality check is essential. For young executives, filled with the excitement of exercising power at progressively more senior levels, no matter how unlikely the above scenario may appear now, it is a wise course to construct the groundwork of ongoing, honest feedback from their management teams, the organization at large and the market beyond. Self-development, whether leaders fear the implications of status and power or revel in it, should focus on learning the preparedness to challenge and be challenged, to work with the implicit contradiction of total self-belief and the acknowledgement of the value of others' contributions.

Fear of failure and fear of success are difficulties rarely discussed in the management literature, more rarely broached in today's corporation where tough regiments of 60-hour working week managers jostle for a crack at a coveted leadership position.

The fears are real enough though. Many a prospective leader, talented, distinguished and confident, has failed in the new job. Colleagues are shocked and puzzled. There seems no explanation. 'A closer study of the dilemma surrounding the fear of failure,' Zaleznik observes, 'indicates that the person has not resolved the concerns he has with competing. It may be that he has adopted or "internalized" unrealistic standards of performance or that he is competing internally with unreachable objects. Therefore he resolves to avoid the game because it is lost before it starts.' (p81)

What are we to say of the fear of success? It seems so improbable. Yet the nearer you move to positions of power and authority and the closer you get to the possibility of stepping into high office yourself, the more you are inclined to worry about its actuality. Zaleznik attributes this to strong feelings of guilt based on a belief that you achieve the position only through displacing someone else. It may also, I suspect, have a good deal to do with an underlying trepidation that you are not up to the job, that you will be 'found out' as a fraud and exposed. I have come across highly successful professionals and executives who, in confidence, said as much. 'I can't understand how I got here,' is the typical admission. 'Other people must know more than me and be better at doing this job.' In the absence of a resolution to such fears, people may sabotage themselves – deliberately, by not following through or by avoiding a crucial decision, or passively, by simply letting things slide, being helpless when success is in sight.

What are the keys to self-development, then?

- Use business realities as the basis of development. Get involved in leading projects, task-forces, and new initiatives. Remember, you will not learn leadership in a classroom.
- Be willing to learn. Continually expand the data-set about yourself by getting accurate feedback: solicit more probing and incisive comment about your performance, particularly in the domain of leadership, grab the chance to go through assessment or development centres – they are tailor-made opportunities for prospective leaders. Finally, learn from your mistakes: what did you do wrong, what did you do right, what could you do differently or better?
- Remember that what has made you successful up until now is not necessarily what will make you successful in a leadership role. Understand the leadership demands on you. Develop yourself to meet and exceed these demands.

- Position yourself for jobs that will make a real difference to your leadership development (not to your career prospects and pay – those will come with leadership attainment). Don't follow the crowd into the popular roles; be objective and take advice.
- Prepare yourself for loneliness. Leadership is authority and will set you apart. People will expect you to lead, not to make friends.
- Take decisions on the basis of rational logic and your convictions. You cannot please everyone. People may be angry with your opinions but they will despise your anxiety and hesitation.
- If you are prepared to challenge, be willing to be challenged. The alternative is to drift ever farther into an uncompromising fanaticism. Let reality check you. Listen to others. Listen to the organization. Listen to the market.
- If you fear failure, or fear success, try to understand why. Are you competing against internal standards that have nothing to do with the actual work? Are you proving something to yourself or doing the work the organization needs? Even the most confident and the most successful of leaders have fears and feelings of ambiguity about the role. If you have similar feelings, remember you're not the first, but if they threaten to immobilize you, you must act. To resolve this you need the assistance of a mentor or coach who can provide objectivity.

Personally I am always ready to learn, although I do not always like being taught.

Winston Churchill
House of Commons, 4 November 1952

Logjams, Prods and External Mentors

One of the downsides of training and one-off development activity is that any positive impact on performance and achievement either does not transfer back to the real work situation or diminishes over time. This is not always true; some training courses or seminars offer insights that change executives forever, but this kind of 'Road to Damascus' experience is rare – how many times

161

has it happened to you? We are filled with good intentions to change and frequently we do, but rarely for long.

Mentoring is a way round this. It is linked to the work managers do. It is action-oriented. It is concerned with personal development geared to solving business and organizational problems practically. Many of the business leaders in this book can point to people who made a difference to their career, in several ways. 'There were probably seven or eight individuals in my career,' says Peter Ellwood, for example, 'who I learned from. They were kind enough to take the time to point out where I should improve. I suppose the common thread I learned from all of them was tenacity and doing your homework, knowing what you're talking about.'

Alex Watson mentions similar assistance:

> A number of managers helped me. In some ways this was to give me space to try things and develop. On the other hand one of my previous bosses pushed me very hard to think about what I had to do to really make progress. He said to me, 'Tell me the three things you're going to concentrate on this year. If you convince me, I'll leave you alone.'

What is interesting though is a point made by Dave Bowyer, that it's usually only later in your career that you realize what the impact of a mentor's help has amounted to, or that you even had mentors at all. Bowyer relates:

> At NCP one particular senior manager approached me and asked me to move to a *smaller* job elsewhere. I thought he was crazy. I couldn't see the point. I asked him why and he just said, 'Trust me'. Nothing else. I did trust him and the move was the right one. He developed me to the pinnacle of the production function.

The idea of mentoring has a long history fraught with various debates, chief among them being the difficulty of satisfactorily matching mentor and protégé. Research tends to show that informal mentoring relationships work best (as we've seen in some of the careers of the business leaders of this book), usually because some managers are better at coaching and advising than others. Obliging all senior managers to take on a formal mentoring role is therefore foolhardy. But should it be left to chance? No. Organizations can do something and so should aspiring leaders.

All too often in the past I have been dismayed to see rising stars fail in the leadership stakes for reasons that could have been avoided or resolved. Some get bogged down in a bigger role and work themselves into a pit, losing sight of the wider business and becoming obsessed with short-term fixes, because no one has been able to see the problem objectively. Others have been moved too soon or too late or have had routes blocked, with no internal mechanisms to identify the logjam and bring authority to bear to break through it.

In these cases there is a good argument to be made for using external mentors (trained coaches or counsellors) to work with targeted managers several times a year. Their role is to act as counsellor, coach, instigator of organizational action, and development resource. They are a prod, if you like, to both the individual (to plan and action relevant development in an ongoing way) and to the organization (to cut bureaucratic red-tape where it is holding up job moves or to expedite internal development action that might involve the individual manager in stretching projects or new initiatives). In this way they become an active custodian of a potential leader's longer term development plan, triggering action that may be forgotten in the heat of day-to-day work, as well as counterbalancing personal development needs with the reality of the organization's business requirements.

In summary:

- Seek out senior managers whom you respect and whose track-record in developing others speaks for itself. Build an informal relationship – it doesn't have to be (perhaps shouldn't be) dignified with the formality of the title 'mentoring' – and seek their advice on business issues and career development.

- Remember that one of the values of a mentor is the network of contacts they can provide, internal and external. They open doors to key jobs or relevant projects. Ultimately, the broader your network and your experience, the more likely you are to understand business better and to learn what matters in leading an organization.

- An organization has few options if it is committed to developing leadership at very senior levels. Training in new styles won't do it. Having a clean-sweep of the management team probably will (remember, it happens sometimes!) and so, short of going down the route of this last option, external mentoring is probably the only way to short-cut leadership development, firstly because it is highly focused on the individual (therefore tailor-made) and secondly because it is externally driven, free from the traditions and prejudices of the firm's corporate culture and emphasizes development towards (I hope) entirely new leadership thinking and behaviour.

- Taking on the role of mentoring is valuable in itself. No one develops as much as the individual who is helping others to develop themselves.
- If your organization offers it, grab the chance of external mentoring. Too many senior managers stop developing themselves, giving the excuse that they have more important matters to worry about. An external mentor provides an outside perspective, enabling you to lift your sights and see beyond the immediate constraints of day-to-day work; leaders *must* learn to do this for themselves, and external mentors can help to start the process and maintain it.
- Beware over-dependence on mentors. It can lead to an executive's downfall. Leadership requires you to stand for your own opinions, to take decisions and risks and live with the consequences. A mentor is an advisor, not a shield behind which you can hide.

Why Leaders Fail to Make it

Morgan McCall Jr and Michael Lombardo reported in 1983 on a study conducted in the US by the Center for Creative Leadership. They worked with several Fortune 500 corporations to understand better why some executives made it to the top and others got close but didn't quite make it.

Derailment or success were usually the result of one of five events or combinations of circumstance, shown in Figure 9.2. The manner in which executives handled these events was a major determining factor of future career success. All senior managers have faults, after all, but some are better than others at handling the complexity, difficulty and stress of the kinds of circumstances mentioned in Figure 9.2. The faults that mattered, none the less, were quite clear. Figure 9.3 summarizes the primary reasons for derailment. The unsuccessful executives usually had only two of the fatal flaws, but they were enough to make the difference. For example, McCall and Lombardo write:

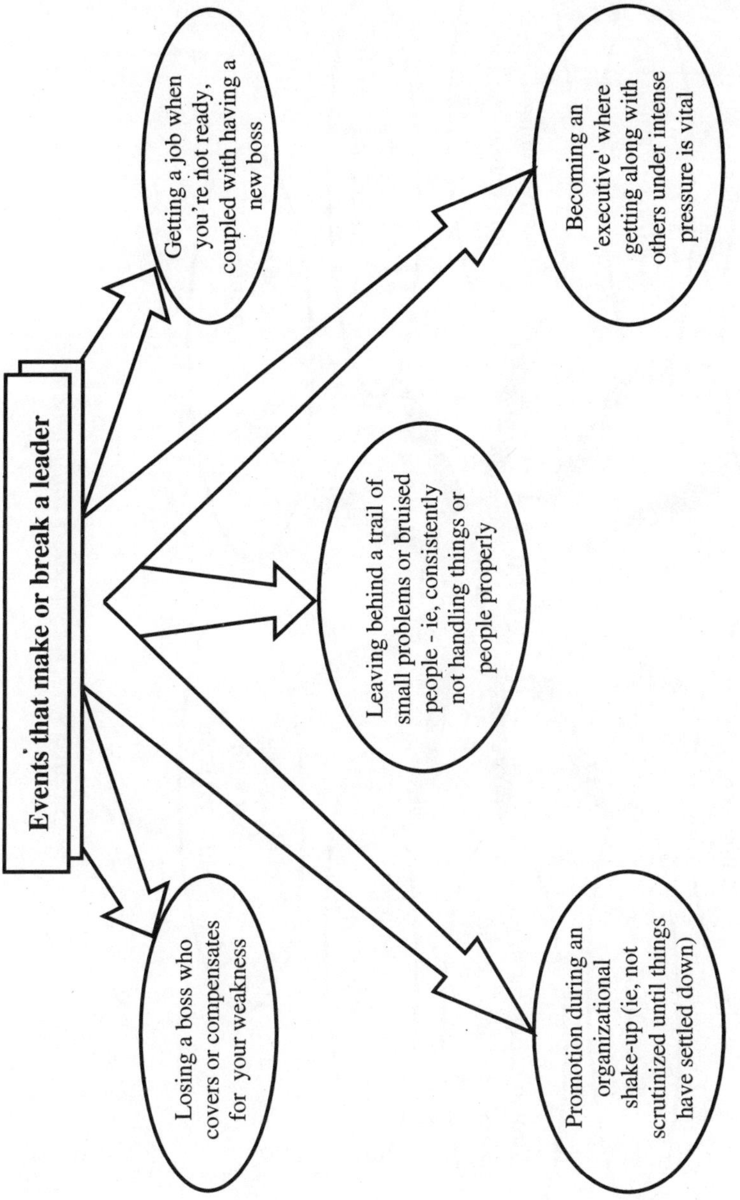
Events that make or break a leader
Losing a boss who covers or compensates for your weakness
Promotion during an organizational shake-up (ie, not scrutinized until things have settled down)
Leaving behind a trail of small problems or bruised people - ie, consistently not handling things or people properly
Getting a job when you're not ready, coupled with having a new boss
Becoming an 'executive' where getting along with others under intense pressure is vital

Figure 9.2 *Making or breaking leaders*

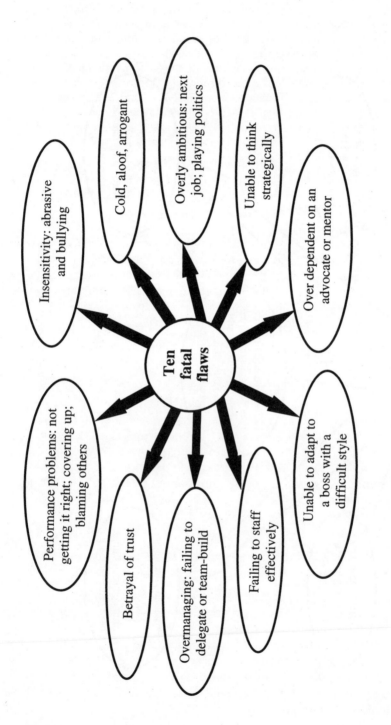

Ten fatal flaws

- Insensitivity: abrasive and bullying
- Cold, aloof, arrogant
- Overly ambitious: next job; playing politics
- Unable to think strategically
- Over dependent on an advocate or mentor
- Performance problems: not getting it right; covering up; blaming others
- Betrayal of trust
- Overmanaging: failing to delegate or team-build
- Failing to staff effectively
- Unable to adapt to a boss with a difficult style

Figure 9.3 *Why leaders fail to make it*

In an incredibly complex and confusing job, being able to trust others absolutely is a necessity. Some committed what is perhaps management's only unforgivable sin – they betrayed a trust. This rarely had anything to do with honesty (which was a given in almost all the cases), rather it was a one-upping of others or a failure to follow through on promises, which wreaked havoc on organizational efficiency. One executive didn't implement a decision as promised, causing conflicts between marketing and production that reverberated downward through four levels of frustrated subordinates.

What is startling (but obvious when you think about it) is that the successful executives and those who didn't quite make it were very similar in certain respects. To get near the top you have to be good at what you do, you must have demonstrated an excellent track-record, and you must have significant accomplishments under your belt. At some point, however, small differences between executives are magnified by the pressure of seniority and the individual's exposure in leadership positions. In short, it's tough at the top. A catastrophic fall from grace is rare. Small differences, as shown in Table 9.1 make winners and losers.

Table 9.1 *Small differences make winners and losers*

All	Those who make it
• Very bright	• Have more diversity in track records
• Identified early	• Maintain composure under stress
• Outstanding track records	• Handle mistakes with poise and grace
• Have a few flaws	• Focus on problems to solve them
• Ambitious	• Get along with all kinds of people – outspoken but not offensive
• Made many sacrifices	

McCall and Lombardo concluded that there were four basic reasons for executive derailment:

- Strengths become weaknesses: loyalty, for example, at more senior levels becomes overdependence; vaulting ambition undermines support.
- Faults eventually come to matter: at some point it is not enough to get by on either interpersonal skills or brilliance alone, for example – you need both.
- Success goes to an executive's head: he or she feels that there is nothing more to learn.

The New Leaders

• Luck: events conspire against even the best – for example, political in-fighting or economic events beyond an executive's control or knowledge.

Morgan W McCall Jr and Michael M Lombardo, *Off the Track: Why and How Successful Executives Get Derailed*. Technical report No. 21, reproduced by permission of the Center for Creative Leadership, Greenboro, NC, © 1983. All rights reserved.

10

THE NEW LEADERS

It Ain't the Way that You do it, It's What You do!

Leadership style, we've been told, is what matters. Be a better leader; change your style; do things differently. Well, I've had my fill of style. If you try to change your leadership style, you're just playing games. It's what you do that matters.

First you have to decide whether you're a leader at all. I wish the list of questions I've given below was a lot shorter. I wish that I could put down a list of five questions you could answer to see whether you really are a leader. But leadership is complex human behaviour. There are no easy questions and there are no easy answers. Try asking these questions of yourself anyway ...

Imposing context

- Can you stand outside your firm and see it as it really is, or are you trapped by your own stake in the past?
- Do you understand the context of your business (where it comes from, what is right and what is wrong with it, where it is strong and where it is weak, and where it is headed)?
- Do you have an organizational vision because it truly means something to you and the people who work for you or because every other firm has one?
- Have you articulated the core of what matters to your business (and what doesn't), what you stand for, what the business stands for, what employees should stand for?
- Do you understand your competition and how to meet and alter it to gain competitive advantage?

Risk making, risk taking

- Are you serving the future of your firm or are you merely a guardian of its past?
- Is command and control more important to you than change and opportunity?
- Can you create psychological space (ie the freedom to act) for yourself?
- Do you actively make risks by seeking opportunities, testing new ideas, pushing authority and freedom to act (and fail) right down the organization?
- Are you prepared to pull the plug on projects that have years and reputations invested in them but which you know are going nowhere?
- Are you willing to make mistakes and take the consequences?

Unpredictability

- Do you create adventure in your organization (or is it all just work)?
- Are you prepared to experiment, induce crises and disturb the tranquil equilibrium of an organization that is doing all right but could do much better? Do you benchmark your processes against the world's best and then go one better?
- Are you and your firm so boringly predictable that your competitors know exactly what you'll do next?
- Are you awaiting disaster before you act (but hoping it doesn't strike in your tenure)?
- Do you obligingly go along every year with the ritual of strategic planning, ignoring and therefore endorsing its blinkered, incrementalist mindset?
- Or are you tackling the tough strategic questions, searching the future for uncharted territory and, instead of relying on what you have inherited, creating your own markets and competitive advantages?

Conviction

- Do you believe in yourself?
- Are your opinions your's or someone else's?
- Do you face up to the problems of your organization honestly or do you prefer to deal with only the good news?
- Can you trust anyone in your team or has your ambition and

the exercise of power so effectively isolated you that you are alone (and vulnerable)?

- Do you thoroughly believe in what you are doing in your firm?

Generating critical mass

- Can you make what you believe in happen?
- Or is the hectic (but frankly comfortable) pace of discussion, endless meetings, conference calls and paperwork sufficient to convince you that you are doing enough – despite the relentless advance of your competitors?
- Are you part of the organizational structure that supresses initiative and destroys the willingness of employees to solve problems in the front-line where it counts?
- Do you seek compliance from employees or their commitment?
- Have you convinced people of the urgency of the need to change, to grab opportunities, to break the conventions and rules of the market and, indeed, to challenge you?

I have asked these and many other implicit questions throughout this book. I have not sought to answer every question that pops up. Indeed, I hope the issues and questions raised here throw up many more. If leaders are asking questions of import, then they are doing their job.

It might seem that the above list of questions, neatly categorized into the five areas of what I have called the leadership domain, are a step-by-step formula for leadership success. Ask the right questions, give the right answers and go to the top of the class. That, of course, is nonsense. Much as we may have been raised in Western society and its institutions to move as rapidly as possible to seek solutions and then implement them, we must, I'm afraid, tackle leadership in a different way. Leadership is developed through the merit of experience and is not simply a collection of new skills. It takes time. It is dependent on many influences and its outcome cannot be guaranteed.

Have We Failed Leadership?

There is no doubt, in my own mind, that the business world (and perhaps the world at large too) has neglected the concept of leadership. Perhaps firms have become frightened in the exercise of power and authority. Perhaps the social–psychological shifts following the Second World War – the crumbling of the old political and social orders and the rebellions of youth in the 1950s and 1960s – have left us ambivalent about leadership. We want strong leaders but we are suspicious of their motives. Perhaps we view leadership with the same sidelong glances that we reserve for autocracy and dictatorship.

Perhaps the very institutions of our Western societies that should be the hothouses of leadership development – our schools, our higher educational facilities – have become too egalitarian to produce the leadership talent that we need. Perhaps the noble goals of impartiality and fairmindedness carry with them the danger of shrinking from competitive encounter and fail us in our need to develop leaders.

Perhaps in the corporate world, for similar reasons, we have mistaken management for leadership. Perhaps we believe it will demean managers and the managerial process if we represent leadership as something *more than* – as different, as possessing an implied higher status.

I have argued strongly in this book that leadership is different. I can see no value in pretending that leaders are not and should not be part of the business world. In fact I think it is more than likely that we shall see a gradual migration to the business world of each nation's brightest and best – rather than to politics or government – as business becomes increasingly global and the challenges, upon which leaders thrive, dwarf the political mêlée they have left behind. And the challenges in business are great indeed. Organizations and whole industries will more and more quickly pass through the cycle of growth, dominance, stability and the threat of decline as their strategies are replicated by competitors (from anywhere in the world) with cheaper labour or by acquiring identical technology or by simple imitation. If you don't believe your industry and your organization are under international threat, think again. Manufacturing has borne the brunt; look at cars, televisions, and commercial aircraft, to name but a few. The services sector has felt the pinch for some time too; accountancy, advertising, car rental, fast food and some forms of banking have been in the forefront.

At such a point the most important and difficult of leadership challenges will confront businesses. They will need to change, to innovate, to reinvent markets, to transform themselves. Leaders will be pushing against forces within their firm that have huge inertia. Functions, divisions, departments, teams – most are walled off from each other. Isolation and focus on highly specific tasks are normal conditions for many employees. Familiarity of systems, procedures, processes, rules, and 'ways of doing things' are much preferable to fluidity or – heaven forbid! – unpredictability. The comfort of nostalgia, of operating with deference to the past, keeps people happy, secure and unchallenged. Information is guarded at the top, filtered at the bottom, lost somewhere in the middle of the organizational hierarchy. The firm chooses as its benchmark comparators those businesses it believes are comparable – the average – and not the world's best. Strategy, as I have lamented elsewhere, is the plan; the plan is the strategy; the firm inches forward while its competitors turn cartwheels.

Where is the force to change? It is certainly 'out there', in the external environment; the (global) needs of customers, the emergence of competitors, the volatile behaviour of the capital markets, the tightening and relaxation of government regulations and the like. This is true, but leaders are the only organizational members who can initiate the action appropriate to respond to such forces. To do so requires from executives behaviour that I have defined as the leadership domain.

How have organizations responded? Some, blessed with genuine leaders in their executive teams, have understood, articulated and imposed a context, at the broadest level, of continual pursuit of competitive advantage, a context of organizational change, upgrading, innovation, and broadening of commercial thinking. Success has come about because the context is accepted by employees as normal and is to be expected. The majority of firms, however, have neglected or failed to impose this context and underlying this failure are failures throughout the leadership domain. Such organizations, I contend, maintain the myth that they value leadership and that they are developing it. Their creation of the myth may not be deliberate – they may, understandably, have been lulled by obedient customers until recent years or be emerging for the first time from the stasis of monopoly – but is this to be forgiven none the less? Will their competitors forgive them? Hardly. Not to understand leadership properly is a failure of leadership in an organization. It will come about because of the comfortable inheritance, self-interest and protectionism of a closed inner circle of executives, who believe they know best and allow no one to challenge their thinking. It will kill off leadership talent in the firm and will eventually kill the firm itself.

What's to be done?

What follows are some suggestions, a distillation, in part, of what has preceded, and a plea for action. The first four are aimed at people who can make a difference in the development of leadership talent in organizations. Chiefs of companies and executive teams – you have the power and the influence to change things and, after all, it is ultimately in your interests. Politicians – you have a role here too, in expanding competition in industry, in curbing protectionism (in some countries to reverse decades-long decline) and in examining and shifting educational policy, at a number of levels, to nurture leaders through constructive individual competition. And finally professionals who advise on training and development in their own organizations, at business schools and across industries – you are uniquely placed to stimulate new thinking and critique in the leadership domain.

My last three suggestions are aimed at the new leaders, at managers who have leadership firmly in their sights, at those who have taken their umpteenth 'leadership' training course and, poor things, are still bewildered by it all, and at students who have the passion and the wherewithal to make a contribution to the future of leadership. *You* have the opportunity.

Chiefs, Politicians and Training and Development Professionals

Spell out the criteria for leadership

I don't mean management. Countless firms have management competencies. Not a few have them set out in great tomes, distributed to every manager in the organization. Many firms actually use these competency lists. Very few have understood or articulated the distinction between management and leadership. People need to know what leadership means. Remove doubt. Tell them. The answers to the following questions will start to spell it out.

What does context mean in your firm? To what extent can managers at different levels get involved in strategy-making? How far will you encourage people to contribute to it and to its communication? How do you encourage disconnection, getting managers to view the firm from outside and to develop an empathy with a broader range of commercial and business models than the one your own organization implicitly understands and accepts – ie outside your industry, outside your home-base?

What do risk and opportunity mean in your firm? What are the limits? How do managers progressively learn about and handle greater levels and types of risk? To what extent are managers expected to go beyond the strategic planning process and explore the future? How are they expected to do this?

How do you drive unpredictability into the business? Which organizations are your best-practice comparators – the world's best, or those that make you look good? To what extent are job moves around the firm encouraged? In what circumstances are experimentation, piloting, and testing endorsed? And what are the ground rules for doing this? What aspects of the firm are sacred, beyond challenge and change? Who is responsible for innovation?

At what point will individual conviction and challenge bring rebuke? To what extent is trust valued?

Is compliance or commitment sought? To what extent are managers challenged and stretched? Are they empowered? What are they empowered to do? And what are the structures and boundaries of their freedom? (There must always be structures and boundaries if freedom is to work.)

Select and develop the best

More advanced skills and capabilities provide higher-order competitive advantage – as long as they are truly more advanced than your competitors'. This is your standard. Make it clear that your promotion and recruitment procedures are geared to getting the very best managers. Then do it. Recruit from the best sources. Use the best assessment methods. People want to see tough (but relevant) entry requirements, no matter what the seniority of candidate. Why should it be different for business unit heads or shopfloor operators?

Promote on merit – which means contribution to the business. And remember, forgive the occasional mistake; leadership is risk.

Compare your management and leadership talent against outstanding competitors

There isn't much more to say on this. If you clearly articulate outstanding examples of managerial and leadership behaviour from other firms as the standard and goal, then people will know what they're shooting for. Some executives will protest vehemently about this. 'Are you saying,' they'll complain, 'that I've got to benchmark myself against executives in another company?' Yes, I am. You will no doubt feel very exposed. The cold wind of competition is blowing straight at you. But the best managers and the best leaders are worrying not only about processes, technology and structures; they're also examining what people do, how they do it, and what they're doing better or differently.

Test and develop leaders against the toughest challenges

Task potential leaders with handling the most demanding customers and customer segments. Get them to know their customers like they know their own organization. Ask them to take on jobs and projects in the most difficult business units. Give them the toughest assignments, particularly assignments which involve leading and managing change and especially in circumstances which demand entirely new thinking or strategic direction. Load up their leadership responsibility by formally packing them off to subsidiaries or other firms for a couple of days a month as independent or non-executive directors. You will not do rising stars any favours by giving them an easy ride through all the high profile (cushy) jobs in the business. Stretch them. If this means rearranging jobs, moving managers around, stepping on toes, so much the better; the change and unpredictability will blow out the cobwebs.

Aspiring Leaders, Students and the Bewildered

Develop yourself

Assume that nobody else will – not withstanding my comments in preceding sections. Gone are the days of organizational paternalism. Moreover, you won't learn leadership on a training course. Anyway, if you need my prompting to develop yourself, you'll never be a leader.

First off, be willing to learn – voraciously acquire knowledge of yourself, of your firm, of the business world, in your current job, in new roles, on assessment centres, whatever. Get involved in business projects and task-forces. Position yourself for the jobs that count, not necessarily the popular jobs. If you're senior enough (or pushy enough), get yourself a non-executive directorship. Remember, however, that what has made you successful thus far may not make you successful in leadership roles, where fear of failure and fear of success are very real dilemmas and where people will expect you to lead rather than please everyone, to have opinions and voice them rather than hesitate, to challenge and be willing to be challenged rather than sliding into fanaticism.

Leverage off others

This is, after all, one of the primary tasks of leaders. Learning via the merit of experience does not mean you should try to do everything yourself. Seek out senior managers who you respect and whose track-record (in business and in developing others) speaks for itself. The relationship needn't be formal, but what matters is that you learn from their accumulated experience and advice. If you are already pretty senior, make use of an external mentor to broaden your thinking and to drive your leadership development, particularly when you are completely embroiled in the day-to-day issues of your job and you need somehow to lift your sights and regain perspective. But heed a warning: a coach or a mentor is an advisor; beware over-dependence.

Act the part

There is an accumulating body of psychological evidence to show that individuals' attitudes and beliefs fall in line with changes to their behaviour – and not, as is commonly held, the other way around. If you are expending all your energy (in classrooms or elsewhere) thinking about being a leader but never behaving like one, you are doomed to stay that way. Leaders are not passive by-standers. Try things. Experiment. Take risks. Change your behaviour. Be a leader.

... And in the End

No one can understand leadership without recognizing that it is, at one and the same time, elusive but momentous, passionate but coldly singleminded, a matter for patience but sudden opportunity, and a force to be grasped by ambitious individuals but nurtured by others. It is a capacity that flourishes in circumstances that may be hopeless, to achieve ends that may be triumphant or forlorn. In a sense it matters little which, for it is the great struggle for victory which is the ordinary habit of leadership.

REFERENCES

Adair, J (1988) *Developing Leaders*, Talbot Adair Press, Guildford.

Adair, J (1990) *Understanding Motivation*, Talbot Adair Press, Guildford.

Adizes, I (1988) *Corporate Lifecycles*, Prentice-Hall, New Jersey.

Argyris, C (1971) *Management and Organizational Development: The path from XA to YB*, McGraw Hill, New York.

Avolio, BJ, Waldman, DA, and Yammarino, FJ (1991) 'Leading in the 1990s: The four I's of transformational leadership'. *Journal of European Industrial Training*, 15 (4), 9–16.

Badaracco, JL, and Ellsworth, RR (1989) *Leadership and the Quest for Integrity*, Harvard Business School Press, Boston.

Bass, BM, and Burger, PC (1979) *Assessment of Managers: An international comparison*, Free Press, New York.

Beer, M, Eisenstat, RA, and Spector, B (1990) *The Critical Path to Corporate Renewal*, Harvard Business School Press, Boston.

Bennis, W (1989) *On Becoming a Leader*, Century Business, London.

Bennis, W, and Nanus, B (1985) *Leaders: The strategies for taking charge*, Harper and Row, New York.

Blake, RR, and Mouton, JS (1966) 'Managerial facades', *Advanced Management Journal*, July.

Business Week (11 September 1978), 'The great congressional power grab', 90–99.

Business Week (25 April 1994), 'That eye-popping executive pay: Is anybody worth this much?', 60–76.

Carroll, P (1993) *Big Blues: The unmaking of IBM*, Orion, London.

Consensus Economics (April 1994). *Consensus Forecasts*, Consensus Economics Inc., London.

Coopers and Lybrand (September 1993). 'Global economic prospects', *UK Economic Outlook*.

Czarniawska-Joerges, B and Wolff, R (1991) 'Leaders on and off the organizational stage', *Organization Studies*, 12 (4), 529–46.

Drucker, P (1977) *Management*, Pan, London.

The Economist (30 October 1993), 'A billion consumers'.

179

The Economist (7 January 1995), 'Pakistan's mighty Khan'.

The Economist (14 January 1995), 'The straining of quality'.

Festinger, L (1957) *A Theory of Cognitive Dissonance*, Stanford, CA.

Fiedler, FE (1976). *A Theory of Leadership Effectiveness*, McGraw Hill, New York.

Forster, EM (1924) *A Passage to India*, Penguin, Harmondsworth.

French, WL, and Bell, CH (1978) *Organization Development*, Prentice-Hall, New Jersey.

Gleick, J (1987) *Chaos: Making a new science*, Viking, New York.

Goss, T, Pascale, R and Athos, A (November–December 1993) 'The reinvention roller coaster: Risking the present for a powerful future'. *Harvard Business Review*, 97–108.

Hamel, G and Prahalad, C K (1994) *Competing for the Future*, Harvard Business School Press, Boston.

Industry Week (15 April 1991), 'CEO pay', 13–18.

Jacques, M (16 January 1995) 'The adulation is over; the drama begins', *The Independent*.

James, L (1994) *The Rise and Fall of the British Empire*, Little, Brown and Co., London.

Janis, IL (1972) *Victims of Groupthink*, Houghton-Mifflin, Boston.

Jones, SG (ed) (1994) *CyberSociety: Computer-mediated communication and community*, Sage, CA.

Kanter, RM (1983) *The Change Masters: Corporate entrepreneurs at work*, Routledge, London.

Kanter, RM (May–June 1990) 'Values and economics' (editorial), *Harvard Business Review*.

Kaplan, RS, and Norton, DP (September–October 1993) 'Putting the balanced scorecard to work', *Harvard Business Review*, 134–47.

King, N (1992) 'Modelling the innovation process: An empirical comparison of approaches', *Journal of Occupational and Organizational Psychology*, 65, 89–100.

Kouzes, JM, and Posner, BZ (1987) *The Leadership Challenge*, Jossey-Bass, San Francisco.

Larwood, L, Kriger, MP, and Falbe, CM (1993) 'Organizational vision: An investigation of the vision construct-in-use of AACSB business school deans', *Group & Organization Management*, 18 (2), 214-236.

Likert, R (1967) *The Human Organization*, McGraw Hill, New York.

Lippitt, GL (1969) *Organization Renewal*, Appleton-Century-Crofts, New York.

Mandela, N (1994) *Long Walk to Freedom: The Autobiography of Nelson Mandela*, Little, Brown and Company, London.

Margerison, CJ (1980) 'How chief executives succeed', *Journal of European Industrial Training*, 4 (5).

Margerison, CJ and Kakabadse, AP (1984) *How American Chief Executives Succeed*, AMA Survey Report, American Management Association.

Marr, A (15 April 1994). 'Wanted: A calm voice above the babble', *The Independent*.

McCall Jr, MW, and Lombardo, MM (1983) *Off the Track: Why and how successful executives get derailed*, Technical Report No. 21, Center for Creative Leadership, North Carolina.

McClelland, DC (1961) *The Achieving Society*, Van Nostrand, New Jersey.

McHugh, P, Merli, G and Wheeler, WA (1995) *Beyond Business Process Reengineering: Towards the holonic enterprise*, Wiley, Chichester.

Mitchell, TR, George-Falvy, J and Crandall, SR (1993) 'Business students' justifications of exceptionally high salaries: Is it OK to make $2 million a year?', *Group & Organization Management*, 18 (4), 500-521.

Mumford, A (1989) *Management Development: Strategies for action*, Institute for Personnel Management, London.

Ohmae, K (1990) *The Borderless World*, Harper Business, New York.

Peters, TJ (1992) *Liberation Management: Necessary disorganization for the nanosecond nineties*, Pan Books, London.

Peters, TJ and Waterman, RH (1982) *In Search of Excellence: Lessons from America's best-run companies*, Warner, New York.

Porter, ME (1990) *The Competitive Advantage of Nations*, The Macmillan Press, London.

Reddin, WJ (1970) *Managerial Effectiveness*, McGraw Hill, New York.

Regan, G (1991) *The Guinness Book of Military Blunders*, Guinness Publishing, Enfield.

Ross, L and Nisbett, RE (1991) *The Person and the Situation: Perspectives of social psychology*, McGraw Hill, New York.

Rotter, JB (1967) 'A new scale for the measurement of interpersonal trust', *Journal of Personality*, 35, 651-65.

Sagan, C and Druyan, A (1992) *Shadows of Forgotten Ancestors: A search for who we are*, Random House, London.

Schroeder, RG, Van de Ven, AH, Scudder, GD and Polley, D (1989) 'The development of innovative ideas', in AH Van de Ven *et al* (eds.) *Research on the Management of Innovation*, Harper and Row, New York.

Semler, R (1993) *Maverick!*, Arrow Books, London.

Sherif, M, Harvey, OJ, White, BJ, Hood, WR and Sherif, CW (1961) *Intergroup Conflict and Cooperation. The Robbers Cave experiment*, University of Oklahoma Book Exchange.

Sherif, M and Sherif, CW (1953) *Groups in Harmony and Tension*, Harper & Row, New York.

Sherif, M, White, BJ and Harvey, OJ (1955) 'Status in experimentally produced groups', *American Journal of Sociology*, 60, 370-9.

Smith, JM (1982) *Evolution Now: A Century after Darwin*, The Macmillan Press, London.

Tajfel, H (November, 1970) 'Experiments in intergroup discrimination', *Scientific American*, 223, 96–102.

Tajfel, H (ed.) (1981) *Human Groups and Social Categories*, Cambridge, University Press.

Thatcher, M (1993) *The Downing Street Years*, Harper Collins, London.

Thomas, R (18 July 1994) 'Best of a bad bunch', *Newsweek*, 26–8.

Tichy, NM and Ulrich, DO (Fall 1984) 'The leadership challenge – A call for the transformational leader', *Sloan Management Review*, 59–68.

Walsh, J (12 July 1993) 'Where have all the leaders gone', *Time*, 17–21.

Walsh, J (5 December 1994) 'The *Time* global 100: Who are the leaders of tomorrow?', *Time*, 22–45.

Westley, F and Mintzberg, H (1989) 'Visionary leadership and strategic management', *Strategic Management Journal*, 10, 17–32.

Yukl, G, Falbe, CM, and Youn, JY (1993) 'Patterns of influence behaviour for managers', *Group & Organization Management*, 18 (1), 5–28.

Zaleznik, A (1989) 'The human dilemmas of leadership', in *People: Managing your most important asset*, Harvard Business Review, Boston.

Zaltman, G, Duncan, R and Holbek, J (1973) *Innovations and Organizations*, Wiley, New York.

Zand, D (1972) 'Trust and managerial problem-solving', *Administrative Science Quarterly*, 17, 229–39.

INDEX